GOD'S
GOT THIS

TIM SHEETS & RACHEL SHAFER

GOD'S GOT THIS

POWER DECREES

to Overcome Problems,

Step Into Purpose, & Receive Promise

DESTINY IMAGE® PUBLISHERS, INC.
P.O. Box 310, Shippensburg, PA 17257-0310
"Promoting Inspired Lives."

This book and all other Destiny Image and Destiny Image Fiction books are available at Christian bookstores and distributors worldwide.

For more information on foreign distributors, call 717-532-3040.

Reach us on the Internet: www.destinyimage.com.

ISBN 13 TP: 978-0-7684-7278-3

ISBN 13 eBook: 978-0-7684-7279-0

For Worldwide Distribution, Printed in the U.S.A.

1 2 3 4 5 6 7 8 / 27 26 25 24 23

DEDICATIONS

Carol and I dedicate this book to our children and grandchildren: Joshua (Jessica) Sheets and their three—Joelle, Samuel, and Grace—and Rachel (Mark) Shafer and their four—Madeline, Lily, Jude, and Jaidin. We pray all of you will always plant the heavens with your word decrees, giving your angels something to work with, and walking out your destinies in God. We could not possibly love any of you any more than we already do, and may you always remember, "God's got this!"

—**Tim Sheets**

To Madeline, Lily, Jude, and Jaidin, you are the inspiration for this book. I pray you will live your lives believing, trusting, and loving God. No matter what comes your way, know He is more than enough for you.

—**Rachel Shafer**

ACKNOWLEDGMENTS

This book happened in a record amount of time. We felt the urgency to place it into the hands of parents and kids as soon as possible. Gratefully, our publisher, Larry Sparks, and Destiny Image felt the same. Giving our angels assignments by decreeing His Word is one of the most important tools we have, and teaching our children "God's Got This" and how to decree is part of the foundation they need to walk out their destinies. Special thanks as always to our "dream team"—Marie Fox, Katelyn Cundiff, and wife/mom, Carol Sheets. They keep us in line, keep things moving, and keep the coffee coming! Our hope is this handbook will become a part of your arsenal for equipping, and we think you will enjoy and learn from it as well!

—**Tim Sheets and Rachel Shafer, Authors**

CONTENTS

Foreword 21

Letter to Parents 25

Introduction 27

Overcome Problems (Ages 0–6th Grade)

1   Sadness 32

2   Afraid 34

3   Feel Like I've Failed 36

4   Peer Pressure 38

5   Feel Worried 40

6   Tough Times 42

7   Feel Angry 44

8   Feel Stressed 46

9   Self-Image (Don't Like How I Look) .48

10   Envy 50

11   Feel Rejected. 52

12   Self-Esteem (Don't Like Myself). 54

13   Worried Things Won't Work Out. 56

14   Making the Right Choice 58

15   Responsibility. 60

16   Comparison 62

17   Discipline 64

18   Changes. 66

19   Doing Unto Others 68

20   Watching My Words. 70

21   Bitterness. 72

22   My Broken Family. 74

23   Lying. 76

24   Keep Making Mistakes. .78

25   Addictive Habits 80

26   Temptation 82

27   Doubt. 84

28   Brokenhearted 86

29   Needing Direction/Guidance 88

30   Feel Disconnected from God. 90

Step into Purpose (Ages 0–6th Grade)

1   Purpose 94

2   Identity 96

3   Destiny. 98

4   Potential 100

5   Chosen. 102

6   Future. 104

7   Friendships 106

8   Worship. 108

9   Witness 110

10   Courage. 112

11   Wisdom. 114

12   Fear of the Lord. 116

13   Knowledge 118

14   Obedience. 120

15   Perseverance 122

16   Serving. 124

17   Consistency 126

18   Thankfulness 128

19   Humility 130

20 Reading the Bible 132

21 Not Too Young. 134

22 Training Your Thoughts. 136

23 Spiritual Authority 138

24 Dreaming Big. 140

25 Guarding Your Heart 142

26 Calling. 144

27 Zeal. 146

28 Peacemakers 148

29 The Power of Prayer 150

30 Living God's Way. 152

Receive Promises (Ages 0 – 6th Grade)

1 God Never Lies 156

2 Holy Spirit 158

3 Fruit of the Spirit. 160

4 Love 162

5 Joy. 164

6 Peace. 166

7 Patience 168

8   Kindness 170

9   Goodness. 172

10   Faithfulness. 174

11   Gentleness. 176

12   Self-Control 178

13   Protection 180

14   Healing 182

15   Hope. 184

16   God Works All for Your Good 186

17   God Will Never Leave You. 188

18   Spiritual Armor 190

19   Angels. 192

20   Grace 194

21   Hearing God's Voice. 196

22   Rainbow Promise 198

23   Strength. 200

24   Overcomer 202

25   Abundant Life 204

26   Redemption 206

27   Forgiveness 208

28   Salvation 210

29   Spiritual Inheritance. 212

30   Heaven. 214

31   Decrees for America. 216

Overcome Problems (Ages 7th Grade–12th Grade)

1   Depression 220

2   Fear. 222

3   Failure. 224

4   Peer Pressure. 226

5   Anxious 228

6   Difficult Circumstances. 230

7   Anger 232

8   Feel Stressed 234

9   Self-Image 236

10   Envy 238

11   Rejection 240

12   Self-Esteem 242

13   Confidence in God. 244

14   Decision Making. 246

15 Responsibility.. 248

16 Comparison 250

17 Discipline 252

18 Changes.. 254

19 Initiative... 256

20 Watching Your Words 258

21 Bitterness.. 260

22 My Broken Family... 262

23 Honesty.. 264

24 Imperfection... 266

25 Addictions... 268

26 Temptation 270

27 Doubt.. 272

28 Broken Heart 274

29 Needing Direction/Guidance 276

30 Feel Disconnected from God................................ 278

Step into Purpose (Ages 7th Grade–12th Grade)

1   Purpose 282

2   Identity 284

3	Destiny	286
4	Potential	288
5	Chosen	290
6	Future	292
7	Friendships	294
8	Worship	296
9	Witness	298
10	Courage	300
11	Wisdom	302
12	Fear of the Lord	304
13	Knowledge	306
14	Obedience	308
15	Perseverance	310
16	Serving	312
17	Consistency	314
18	Thankfulness	316
19	Humility	318
20	Reading the Bible	320
21	Not Too Young	322
22	Training Your Thoughts	324

23 Spiritual Authority 326

24 Dreaming Big 328

25 Guarding Your Heart 330

26 Calling 332

27 Zeal 334

28 Peacemakers 336

29 The Power of Prayer 338

30 Living God's Way 340

Receive Promises (Ages 7th Grade–12th Grade)

1   God Never Lies 344

2   Holy Spirit 346

3   Fruit of the Spirit 348

4   Love 350

5   Joy 352

6   Peace 354

7   Patience 356

8   Kindness 358

9   Goodness 360

10 Faithfulness 362

11	Gentleness	364
12	Self-Control	366
13	Protection	368
14	Healing	370
15	Hope	372
16	God Works All for Your Good	374
17	God Will Never Leave You	376
18	Spiritual Armor	378
19	Angels	380
20	Grace	382
21	Hearing God's Voice	384
22	Rainbow Promise	386
23	Strength	388
24	Overcomer	390
25	Abundant Life	392
26	Redemption	394
27	Forgiveness	396
28	Salvation	398
29	Spiritual Inheritance	400
30	Heaven	402

31 Decrees for America 404

About Dr. Tim Sheets 407

About Rachel Shafer................................... 409

Contact Information for Tim Sheets..................... 411

Contact Information for Rachel Shafer.................. 413

FOREWORD

As parents of five children, we are contending for revival in our nation, and we recognize the tremendous value this book carries. We love the Sheets family and honor the impact they have made in our nation through their leadership and their apostolic decrees. Now, they have answered the assignment to decree a shift in the lives of our youth. We have seen how biblical decrees can shift hopeless situations into victory stories, and we have no doubt there will be victory stories that will come from this book.

The Bible promises in Job 22:28 that if we decree a thing, it will be established. When we allow the Word of God to renew our minds, a transformation to our thoughts and words takes place. Therefore, authority and power are released in the decrees of those who renew their minds by God's Word. It is imperative that we allow the Bible, not culture, to be the ultimate authority and influence in our lives. Only then will we be empowered to properly decree and lead our generation into righteousness that is solely found in Jesus Christ. It is time to decree and establish a generation for Jesus!

We have witnessed how Carol, Tim, and Rachel continue to contend for their children and for this generation. We have also witnessed the miracles that have been birthed through their unwavering faith. As revivalists, our personal lives have been impacted by the ministry and apostolic decrees of Tim Sheets and his family. Through their ministry, we have been fueled with faith to keep contending for revival in our nation.

Apostle Tim Sheets carries a sharp anointing to discern the times and seasons we are in, and the strategic decrees needed to bring breakthrough. He is able to do this because he is a friend of God. Biblical decrees are like weapons in the hands of a warrior. In the Bible, the Apostle Paul knew the power of decrees, and Paul instructed young Timothy to wage war with the prophetic decrees spoken over him (see 1 Timothy 1:18). In like manner, Apostle Sheets and his family instruct and exemplify the power of decrees to our generation. The Sheets family has had a major role in positively shifting the course of our nation through Holy Spirit-led decrees, and Tim continues to do so regularly throughout the land of America.

Now, you and I have the privilege to join our voices with the Sheets family by making Spirit-led, biblical decrees over our children and the youth of this generation to see breakthroughs in their lives. This book contains strategic decrees that will release victory in the areas that are most challenging for our children and youth. Through this book, you and your family will be equipped to identify areas under attack and the necessary weapons of decree to defeat the enemy in their lives. There are over 180 decrees that will establish victory in your children's lives! We will witness victory in this generation's mental health, identity, freedom, destiny, and purpose in Christ Jesus!

We believe your family will be blessed by these prayers and focused decrees for your children's futures. Whether or not you have children, this book equips you to take part in shaping the next generation through your prayers. There is a battle for our youth and their identity, and the Sheets family is on the front lines fighting for the future of our youth. By actively reading and applying the principles in this book, you too will join the front lines of victory for the children and youth of this generation.

—**Tommy & Miriam Evans**
Revivalists
Authors of
Decrees That Unlock Heaven's Power **and** *Glory Miracle*

LETTER TO PARENTS

Dear Parents,

As a mom, I'll be there for my children as much and as often as possible, but for all the times I cannot, I want my children to be prepared. They need to be emboldened and empowered to know who they are in Christ. They must know their purpose and identity are found in God.

This book will help prepare kids to handle the attacks and the enemy's agenda without them being blindsided. God's Word is filled with guidance, answers and ways to equip them. It is vital they know what God has to say and how to apply and decree it over their lives.

It is important for kids to know they are who God says they are. He has an amazing, beautiful plan written for their lives and wants to help them fulfill their purpose and destiny. Part of our responsibility as parents is to partner with God in guiding and helping them to see His purpose for them.

I pray this book is a valuable tool to inspire and prepare kids to be equipped and ready to live a Spirit-filled life. If your children are younger, I encourage you to read through these devotionals and decrees with them, making sure they fully understand. I know it will lead to beneficial and meaningful conversations. I pray your children are empowered to believe, no matter what the situation, God's got this!

Blessings!

Rachel Shafer

INTRODUCTION

There is a war going on for control of the hearts and minds of our children. It is a conscious effort to indoctrinate our kids with antichrist values that eat away at the moral platforms upon which "a good life" has been built for centuries. Many of our schools and universities are openly teaching demon doctrines. Even the traditional sexual identity of human beings is being redefined. We are being encouraged to identify with whatever pronoun we want— he, she, they, ze—as gender confusion is declared as normal behavior. Our children's minds are being bombarded daily with nonsense and lies. Alarmed parents are being told to "stay out of it; we will teach your kids what they need to know." Even the definition of a woman or a mother is seemingly beyond the level of some tenured professors. They don't know! How crazy!

If the scenarios that are rampant in today's culture are confusing to those with common sense, can you imagine what they are doing to our children? We must do something to change the mess in our education system. And we must also do what God told Moses during the Exodus: "Teach My Word to your children. Explain My ways to them. Talk about them in your homes. Go over My sayings with them as you're walking along life's pathways. Then they will have good success" (my paraphrase of Deuteronomy 11:18-21 and Joshua 1:8)

The wise King Solomon put it succinctly in Proverbs 22:6 (NCV): *"Train children to live the right way, and when they are old, they will not stray from it."* The Message Bible is shouting this verse into our times: *"Point your kids in the right direction—when they're old they won't be lost."* We must point our kids in the right direction; the tried-and-true direction is God's way.

This is the reason we wrote this book. It will help point children to God's way, using stories and examples from the Bible. Each topic is written about in an age-appropriate way, and you will be able to use the devotionals to discuss God's Word in practical ways, in order to help your children apply His Word to their lives. Biblical decrees are statements of what we believe based on God's Word, promises, wills, or ways. Job 22:28 (KJV) says you will *"decree a thing,"* and it will *"be established."* The word *thing* is the Hebrew word *omer*, which means *speech, word, or promise.* Declare God's promises. Declare His Word. Speak what His words say, and they will be established.

We have listed decrees of faith for each topic in this book. Speak them, think about them, pray about them, and they will renew your children's thinking to align with what God says concerning true identity, purpose, and destiny. The decrees will also instruct your children on how to know God's will and plan for their lives, how to hear God's voice, how to live a morally sound life, how to be who God made them to be, how to be successful, what it means to know God as Father, how angels assist them, and more lessons and truths that will help build a solid foundation upon which your children can mature and grow.

Decrees of faith help reinforce a consistent principle throughout the Bible, and that is the importance of our words! Our children must understand this as it is key to them becoming who God says they can be. Proverbs 18:21 (NKJV) tells us, *"Death and life are in the power of the tongue."* Job 6:25 (NKJV) says, *"How forceful are right words!"* This truth was emphasized to me years ago. I was reading Genesis 1, concerning the awesome description of God creating the heavens and the earth. Suddenly, I clearly heard the voice of Holy Spirit saying, "Words are seeds." His voice was heavy with meaning and instruction. I have read Genesis 1, which was penned by Moses thousands of years ago, countless times. But this time, I leaned back from my desk and echoed aloud what was recorded in ancient history all those long years ago: "Words are seeds." I knew Holy Spirit was giving me a truth that is still alive, still powerful, and still needs to be loosed today. It was a moment of enlightenment, and I would never be the same after that revelation.

Words are seeds that germinate and grow. When planted properly, word seeds reproduce themselves. They are the concealed beginnings of something that can grow to fullness when we believe and act upon them.

Decrees are word seeds that we plant into our lives. This book will equip your children with good word seeds (decrees and declarations) that they can speak aloud and grow into God's promises for their lives. These word seeds will become an abundant harvest that your children can live on when they become adults.

Let's start planting good seeds!

—**Tim Sheets**

OVERCOME PROBLEMS

(Ages 0–6th Grade)

1 SADNESS

"You changed my sorrow into dancing."
(Psalm 30:11 NCV)

Sometimes you will have days that are sad. Someone may say something mean to you, a family member may be sick, or you may lose a loved one. Sad things happen to everyone, but if you are a Christian, you always have someone you can talk to who cares about you: Jesus!

David had many times of sadness and the Bible says that sometimes he cried all night long. Everything changed for David when he started talking to God. David asked God to help him and God did!

God makes things better, giving you someone to talk to who is there for you. He also reminds you that He can do anything. God promises to change your sadness into joy.

When you are feeling sad, talk to God about it, read your Bible, and worship Him. As you do, you will begin to feel His presence filling you with joy.

My Decrees

- I decree that You are with me at all times, the good and the bad, and no matter how I feel, You invite me to give it over to You.

- I decree that I trust You with everything, knowing if it matters to me, it matters to You.

- I declare that You are stepping into my situation and I trust You are taking care of me.

- Thank You for always understanding me and always being with me.

2 AFRAID

"Don't be afraid, for I am with you."
(Isaiah 41:10 NLT)

Have you ever gone outside and played in the rain? On a warm day, enjoying the rain can be so much fun! Sometimes though, rain can also bring lightning and thunder. You may not feel afraid of storms during the day, but at night when you're alone and trying to sleep, you might feel nervous and fearful.

When I was young, if I became afraid of something, I would go to my parents' room. It helped me not to feel frightened because I could see that my parents weren't afraid.

God isn't afraid of anything and He is always with you. When you became a Christian, you received the gift of the Holy Spirit and the Holy Spirit is God. That means God is with you wherever you are and He will help you not to feel afraid. He will calm your fears.

My Decrees

- I decree that I will be strong and courageous and I am brave because Jesus lives in me.

- I declare that You are my hiding place and You never leave or forsake me.

- I decree that angels are all around me and fear has to go, in the Name of Jesus!

- I thank You that fear has no hold on me.

3 FEEL LIKE I'VE FAILED

"This is what the Lord says: 'When a man falls down, doesn't he get up again? And when a man goes the wrong way, doesn't he come back again?'"
(Jeremiah 8:4 ICB)

Did you know the first popsicle ever made was actually a mistake? An 11-year-old boy named Frank Epperson wanted to make his own soda. He filled a cup with powdered soda, water, and a stirring stick. He left his mixture outside overnight and it became the very first popsicle! He decided he liked his mistake so much that he continued making the frozen treats. He first called the treats the "Eppsicle" after his name. His children started calling them "Pop's sicle," which led to the famous popsicle name. What started out as a failure turned into great success!

Sometimes things you try may not work and that's okay. If you fall down, do you stay on the ground? Of course not! You get back up. If you're having trouble with something, don't give up! Give it to God. He can help turn any failure into success.

Think About It
What should I do if I feel like giving up?

My Decrees

- I decree that God never gives up on me so I won't give up on myself either!

- I declare that I can do all things because You live in me and Your love never fails.

- I declare that You can turn my failure into success.

- I thank You for "fresh starts" and for always being there to pick me up if I stumble or fall.

4 PEER PRESSURE

"Don't copy the behavior and customs of this world, but let God transform you into a new person by changing the way you think. Then you will learn to know God's will for you, which is good and pleasing and perfect."
(Romans 12:2 NLT)

Has anyone ever said to you, "Just because everyone is doing it doesn't make it a good idea?" Peer pressure means doing something just because everyone else is.

There can be positive peer pressure. For example, your friends study and make good grades and that makes you want to improve your study habits too. That's a great thing! But often, peer pressure is negative. A lot of people may be doing something you know is a bad idea, but you don't want to feel left out. An example of this is if a group of kids are calling someone names and they want you to join them. You know it's wrong, but you want to be included. What that group of kids are doing is negative peer pressure.

The Bible says not to copy the behavior of the world, but to make wise decisions. A big part of this is not to do what everyone else is doing but to make your own choice based on what you know to be right. God doesn't want you to do what everyone else is doing; He wants you to live for Him.

My Decrees

- I decree that You give me power to do the right thing and make the right choices.

- I believe You help me make good decisions that will please You.

- I declare that You are my strength and my guide in everything I do.

- I decree that I will always choose to do what honors You.

- Thank You for giving me the strength to follow You no matter what others say.

5 FEEL WORRIED

"Don't worry about anything; instead, pray about everything. Tell God what you need, and thank him for all he has done."
(Philippians 4:6 NLT)

In life you have things you worry about. You worry about being liked by people, who you'll sit with at lunch, whether you'll pass a test, or if you'll be good on a sports team. Some worries seem bigger than others. Some people worry about being sick or being safe. But Jesus tells you not to worry.

Worries can weigh you down and keep you from being the person God wants you to be. Have you ever carried your backpack home from school and it was filled with books because you had homework? I bet the backpack was very heavy! However, as you emptied the bag, it became much lighter.

Although worries aren't heavy books in a backpack, they can still feel like they weigh you down. When you worry, you're not letting God take care of things. Jesus tells us we can trust Him and He always keeps His promises. Pray and give your worries to God.

My Decrees

- I decree that I will place my worries in Your Hands.

- I decree that I will not try to fix everything myself. I will trust You.

- I will listen for Your voice and refuse to listen to the voice of the enemy who tries to put thoughts in my mind and heart to keep me upset.

- I declare that You are with me and You are my problem solver.

- Thank You for being my peace.

6 TOUGH TIMES

"You meant to hurt me, but God turned your evil into good."
(Genesis 50:20 NCV)

Do you ever have days where things just aren't going right? You lost your homework, couldn't find one of your shoes, and found out your mom was making your least favorite meal for dinner. Perhaps your days feel really hard because a bully won't leave you alone at school, your best friend is mad at you, or your parents are fighting. If you are facing a tough time, remember God is bigger and He knows how to help you find the good things even when things seem bad.

God uses tough times in our lives to change us and make us more like Him. For example, He could use the bully who won't leave you alone to help you know how to be a good friend. Or He could use the sadness of your parents fighting to help you learn that your trust and hope is in Jesus.

I know this might be really hard to understand, but God is good in everything He does. Trust Him. He knows and sees every tough time that comes your way. Remember, *"God even knows how many hairs are on your head"* (Matthew 10:30 ICB). So, He definitely cares about the bigger things in your life!

Think About It

How can I see the good when things seem bad?

My Decrees

- I decree that when things in my life are tough I will keep my eyes on You.

- I declare that You are always with me and I trust You.

- I decree that my faith is in You and You are turning things around.

- Thank You that when someone tries to harm me, You will turn it for my good.

7 FEEL ANGRY

"Always be willing to listen and slow to speak.
Do not become angry easily, because anger will
not help you live a good life as God wants."
(James 1:19-20 ICB)

Do you ever get so mad you could kick a wall? Or punch a pillow? Have you ever gotten so mad that your face felt hot and you couldn't think straight? Those are all signs of anger. The Bible tells us that anger itself is not a sin, but if we let anger control us and do bad things because of it, then it is sin (see Ephesians 4:26).

Anger must be controlled so you don't harm yourself or others. The Bible says to be slow to anger. Everyone gets mad sometimes, but you have to be slow to anger, so your emotions don't get out of control. When you get angry, you should stop and walk away. Feelings don't last forever, but what you do with those feelings might. Pray and ask God to help you calm down. Remember, He wants you to live a good life and He is always there to help you.

Think About It
What can you do to deal with being angry?

My Decrees

- I decree that anger does not control me.

- I declare that I will speak Your Word over my life and think on things that are good and pure until I feel calm.

- I decree that I will not act out my angry feelings.

- Thank You for helping me speak words of peace and not words of anger.

8 FEEL STRESSED

"Cast all your anxiety on him
because he cares for you."
(1 Peter 5:7 NIV)

Stress is what you feel when you are worried, uncomfortable about something, or anxious. This worry in your mind can make your body feel bad. You may feel angry, frustrated, scared, or afraid—which can give you a stomachache or a headache.[1] Do any of these things sound like something God wants for you? Of course not!

Sometimes you might feel extra nervous about taking a test at school. Or you might be really worried about facing your friends after a fight. If you begin to feel stressed and upset about something, talk to God about it. You don't have to handle everything on your own. In fact, God wants you to give your concerns to Him because He cares so much for you! Remember, worrying doesn't accomplish anything, but praying does. God doesn't want you to feel troubled. When you pray, He will fill you with peace. Life is easier to manage when you keep your eyes on Him.

Think About It
Why does God care about your worries?

My Decrees

- I decree that You are with me no matter what I am facing. I am never alone.

- I declare that I will talk to You about everything I'm going through and give You all my worries, problems, and fears.

- I declare that You are bigger than anything I face and Your strength and help will see me through!

- Thank You that I do not have to walk in stress because You care for me.

9 SELF-IMAGE
(DON'T LIKE HOW I LOOK)

"But God told Samuel, "Looks aren't everything. Don't be impressed with his looks and stature. . . . God judges persons differently than humans do. Men and women look at the face; God looks into the heart."
(1 Samuel 16:7 MSG)

There may be things about your appearance that you don't like and wish you could change. It is important to know you are God's masterpiece and He created you beautiful and unique. You are beautiful because you were created in the image of God.

Psalm 139:14 (NKJV) says you are *"fearfully and wonderfully made."* Nothing can change that! Healthy eating, getting enough rest, and exercising regularly are great ways to take care of the body God created for you. You should show thankfulness and respect for what God has created by treating yourself with care. While you should keep your body healthy, God is more concerned with what's inside you. He wants you to keep your heart and mind focused on Him so that you become a true reflection of who He is. See yourself as God sees you: a beautiful, wonderful masterpiece.

Think About It
How can you see yourself as God sees you?

My Decrees

- I decree that I am made for You and by You and You love me no matter what.

- I declare that I will take care of my body and practice good hygiene and I will take care of all the things I can control.

- I decree that I will look to You to help me take care of the "inside" by guarding my heart and spirit to represent You.

- Thank You for helping me see myself the way You see me.

10 ENVY

"Let us not become conceited, provoking or envying each other."
(Galatians 5:26 NIV)

Have you ever had a friend show you a brand-new gift he received and it made you feel upset? Or you found out your sister got invited to go somewhere and you became angry because you weren't? Envy is when you feel unhappy because you want what someone else has. Being envious does not glorify God and one of His Ten Commandments says, "You shall not covet." That means that you shouldn't want what someone else has.

A great way to overcome any feelings of envy is by remembering things you are thankful for. You may not have the biggest house, the newest toys or clothes, but be thankful for what you do have. If you are feeling envious over what someone else has, you can ask God to help you feel thankful instead.

Think About It

Why do you think God doesn't want us to wish for what other people have?

My Decrees

- I decree that I will not compare myself to others but feel confident in how You made me and what You have done for me.

- I decree that I will be happy for others and trust You to take care of me.

- I declare that I will not allow jealousy to have any place in my heart.

- Thank You for everything You have blessed me with.

11

FEEL
REJECTED

*"I prayed to the Lord, and he answered
me. He freed me from all my fears."*
(Psalm 34:4 NLT)

It can be hard to want something so badly but then not get it. Maybe you really wanted a spot on the soccer team or a solo in the school musical, but you didn't get it. Rejection can make you feel sad or disappointed and it's okay to feel those emotions. But God doesn't want you to think about the bad feelings for long. If you are rejected for a position on the team, you may feel like you will never be picked and that is when fear may take over your thoughts. One rejection doesn't mean you should give up on your hopes and wants.

When you are faced with a hurtful situation it's important to remember the truth. There will be other opportunities for you. Psalm 34:4 says the Lord will free you from any fear and bad feelings when you pray to Him. God will always love you and He will always be there for you.

My Decrees

- I decree that when I feel disappointed I will trust You to direct my path.

- I decree that Your love is more than enough for me.

- I declare that giving up is not an option for me and I will not allow rejection or fear to live in me.

- I decree that I will keep moving forward and know You have a plan for me that cannot be stopped.

- Thank You for Your unconditional love and acceptance.

SELF-ESTEEM
(DON'T LIKE MYSELF)

"'And you must love the Lord your God with all your heart, all your soul, all your mind, and all your strength.' The second is equally important: 'Love your neighbor as yourself.' No other commandment is greater than these."
(Mark 12:30–31 NLT)

This Bible verse clearly says to love God with all your heart. It also says to love your neighbor as yourself. Have you ever thought about what it means to love yourself?

Self-esteem is when you are confident in who you are and what you can do. It is easy to get self-esteem wrong, though. You don't want to think too highly of yourself, but you also don't want to think badly of yourself.

It is important to know and be confident in who you are in Christ, not in your abilities. This can be a struggle even for people who seem like they have it all together. For example, the person who is always getting good grades at school may feel like, if they don't get those grades, they aren't good enough. You should want to try your best but know your worth and value come from God, not by how well you do something.

God's love for you doesn't change based on whether you are the smartest or best. He loves you no matter what.

Think About It
Why does God love you?

My Decrees

- I decree that I am created by You and for You.

- I declare that I will treat myself with love and respect.

- I declare that I am confident because of You, not because of things I may do.

- I decree that You work in me and through me.

- I thank You that Your love never gives up on me.

13 WORRIED THINGS WON'T WORK OUT

"And I am certain that God, who began the good work within you, will continue his work until it is finally finished on the day when Christ Jesus returns."
(Philippians 1:6 NLT)

Sometimes you may doubt God, especially in tough times. There are many examples in the Bible of times when people doubted God. In Mark 4, Jesus told His disciples He wanted to go to the other side of a large sea. As they were going across the large body of water, Jesus fell asleep in the boat. The wind and the waves began to get very strong as a storm began and the disciples were afraid their boat was going to sink. They woke Jesus up and asked Him if He cared they were going to drown. Jesus got up and told the storm to be still and it obeyed! The disciples couldn't believe the wind and the waves listened to God's voice!

When God wants you to do something you can be confident that He will see His plans fulfilled. He will always be there for you. Live confidently in the life God has planned for you.

Think About It

**Can you think of a time when
God has been there for you?**

My Decrees

- I decree that You know right where I am and You will always meet me there.

- I declare that You order my steps, and even when I can't see it, You are working everything out.

- I declare that my trust is in You and I can lay any worries I have at Your feet. You are good all the time.

- Thank You for taking me through tough times.

14 MAKING THE RIGHT CHOICE

"Seek his will in all you do, and he will show you which path to take."
(Proverbs 3:6 NLT)

You make choices every day: whether or not to brush your teeth, how to fill your time, or whether or not to read your Bible or clean your room. There are other choices that may be a little harder to make, such as if you should watch that show at your friend's house or stand up for the person being bullied at school. Sometimes it can be difficult to know what to choose. No matter what, the choices you make always have consequences, good or bad.

As a believer in Jesus, you want to follow Him and make the types of decisions He would make. You might be wondering how you can do that. When you fix your thoughts on what is true, good, and pure, you make your choice based on God's standards. You're actually training your mind to think about the right things so, when you are faced with a choice, you will know what to do. You can also pray and ask God to help you. Keep your mind on the things of God and you will make the right choice.

Think About It
What will help you make the right choice?

My Decrees

- I decree that I will guard my heart and fill my mind with Your Word so that I will be strong to make good choices in my life.

- I declare that I will not be afraid to do the right thing when faced with a decision regarding right or wrong.

- I decree that You are in me so I have what it takes to live for You.

- Thank You for leading me on the right path and being an on-time God.

15 RESPONSIBILITY

"The master said, 'Well done, my good and faithful servant. You have been faithful in handling this small amount, so now I will give you many more responsibilities. Let's celebrate together!'"
(Matthew 25:23 NLT)

D o you have any tasks at home that you are in charge of? Do you take out the trash, clean your room, or do the dishes? These are all examples of responsibility.

It's not always fun to be in charge of something, but an important part of growing up is learning how to take care of things you've been given. Most responsibilities come from blessings. God gave you your teeth, so brushing your teeth every day is a great way to take care of something God has given you.

Being responsible isn't just about how you care for your stuff; it is also about how you choose to act. God wants you to take charge of your behavior too. He wants you to be obedient, kind, loving, and helpful. The Bible says if you are responsible with a small amount, God will give you more. That's pretty awesome! God has given you so much and one of the best ways you can thank Him is to be responsible.

My Decrees

- I decree that I will be faithful and responsible with all God has put in my life.

- I declare that I will be obedient in the big and small things.

- I declare that I will be responsible for my actions and attitude and will do my best to be loving, kind, and helpful.

- Thank You for trusting me.

16 COMPARISON

"Oh, don't worry; we wouldn't dare say that we are as wonderful as these other men who tell you how important they are! But they are only comparing themselves with each other, using themselves as the standard of measurement. How ignorant!"
(2 Corinthians 10:12 NLT)

Comparison is when you are looking for similarities or differences between items. You may be grocery shopping with your mom, watching her read the labels on two different soup cans. She is trying to decide which soup is healthier for her family. Comparison can be good in an example like this, but it can be negative if you are comparing yourself with others. Whether it is physical appearance, abilities, or what someone has, comparison is rarely good.

The Bible says that in every circumstance you are to be content. Content means being happy with what you have. If you are comparing yourself with what someone else has, you are no longer content with the blessings God has given you. A way not to compare yourself with others is to ask God for the strength to overcome the desire to compare. You don't have to live your life trying to be like others. God loves you and thinks you're awesome!

Think About It

How can Jesus help you not compare yourself to others?

My Decrees

- I decree that I will not compare my life, who I am and what I have, to any other person.

- I declare that You designed me and You are working in me to be the best I can be.

- I declare that I will be content and happy for others as You are working in them.

- I am thankful for every blessing You give!

DISCIPLINE

"No discipline is enjoyable while it is happening—it's painful! But afterward there will be a peaceful harvest of right living for those who are trained in this way."
(Hebrews 12:11 NLT)

I bet you have rules to follow at your house. I'm also guessing if you don't follow those rules, there will be consequences. It's definitely not fun to be grounded or have a privilege taken away, but these are ways your parents show they love you. It wouldn't be safe or healthy for your parents to let you do whatever you wanted. What if they never told you *not* to touch a hot stove? And then when you did and burned yourself, they just said, "Oh well, now you know."

It may not be enjoyable to hear, "No," or "Don't do that," but your parents tell you these things out of love and for your protection. It is the same way with God. He teaches you how to live through His Word. When you follow His way of doing things, your life will go more smoothly. Remember, He only wants what is best for you!

Think About It
What are some ways you can follow God's rules?

My Decrees

- I decree that I will listen and obey!

- I declare that I will be teachable and do things Your way. You are the best trainer!

- I declare that I will trust Your work in my life, knowing You will be with me every step of the way.

- Thank You for always wanting what's best for me.

18 CHANGES

"So don't worry about these things, saying, 'What will we eat? What will we drink? What will we wear?' These things dominate the thoughts of unbelievers, but your heavenly Father already knows all your needs. Seek the Kingdom of God above all else, and live righteously, and he will give you everything you need."
(Matthew 6:31-33 NLT)

Life is filled with change. You switch to a different grade each year, which may mean new teachers, new friends, or perhaps a new school. Maybe you've had an even bigger change by moving to a new area or dealing with something unfamiliar. The Bible gives several keys in dealing with change in the opening verses from Matthew 6. Whenever you face a change, you want to be sure that you're going to be okay. The very first verse lets you know Jesus understands basic worries. He starts with food, drink and clothing. The verse goes on to say He already knows your needs. You don't have to worry because God knows.

God doesn't promise a problem-free life, but He does promise He knows what you're going through. Whenever everything feels like it's unknown and changing, you can depend on God. He knows the changes, and when you seek Him, He will be there for you.

Think About It

How can I trust God through changes?

My Decrees

- I decree that I will not fear change and I will be strong knowing You are looking out for me.

- I declare that You supply every need I have and no matter what changes are taking place You go before me.

- I declare that I am not afraid!

- Thank You for being with me in every change.

DOING UNTO OTHERS

"Suppose you see a brother or sister who has no food or clothing, and you say, 'Good-bye and have a good day; stay warm and eat well'— but then you don't give that person any food or clothing. What good does that do?"
(James 2:15-16 NLT)

God wants you to be the type of person who makes things happen— the kind of person who sees a problem and then takes action to try and solve it. Simple examples of this would be to empty the trash can if it were full, or wash the dishes you notice are left in the sink.

Now, there are many problems in the world that can seem overwhelming, but the point is to try and figure out what you can do, not think about what you can't do. Of course, you know you can pray, but you can also take action like the verse in James says. You could even be the answer to your own prayer.

If you see someone at school or church who doesn't have a friend, go be friendly to them. If you see your neighbor struggling to get their door open while carrying in groceries, go open the door. Ask your parents if you can have a lemonade stand and send the money you make to those in need or volunteer in some way. God loves to use His people to make the world a better place. Take the initiative, and make good things happen!

Think About It
What are some things you could do for others?

My Decrees

- I decree that I will look for ways to help others every day.

- I decree that I will be the person who steps up, even in the smallest ways.

- I declare that You will use me to be a blessing to others and You will open my eyes to those around me whom I can help.

- I decree that I will do for others what I would like others to do for me.

- Thank You for using me to bless others.

20 WATCHING MY WORDS

"Words kill, words give life; they're either poison or fruit—you choose."
(Proverbs 18:21 MSG)

God created you with a tongue and it is an important part of your body. A tongue helps you eat and speak. When tongues are used to speak, they are very powerful. When I was little there was a saying, "Sticks and stones may break my bones, but words can never hurt me." But that's not true. Words can hurt a lot.

Have you ever been hurt by someone's words? Or maybe you've done the hurting? The opening verse in Proverbs says your words can kill or give life. This means your words can cause damage, as in making someone feel sad, angry, helpless, or upset. Or your words can give joy, making someone feel happy, calm, hopeful, or peaceful.

Luke 6:45 (NKJV) says, *"Out of the abundance of the heart [the] mouth speaks."* Fill your heart with the truth of God's Word so that you speak words of life.

My Decrees

- I decree that I will use my words for good. I will use them to be a blessing.

- I decree that I will use my words to build others up, not tear them down.

- I declare that I will speak life-giving words, not words that destroy others.

- Thank You for helping me choose right words.

21 BITTERNESS

"Get rid of all bitterness, rage, anger, harsh words, and slander, as well as all types of evil behavior."
(Ephesians 4:31 NLT)

Have you ever had something happen to you that made you sad or angry? Maybe someone embarrassed you or said something hurtful to you. When people hurt you, seeds are planted. If the bad seeds are allowed to grow, they become roots of bitterness.

Bitterness can also be thought of as "holding a grudge." Has anyone ever done something to you and whenever you think of that person you feel hurt or angry all over again? If so, that is bitterness. The Bible says to get rid of all bitterness. You do that by forgiving the person who hurt you. Forgiveness can be hard to do but you can pray and ask God to remove unforgiveness from your heart and replace it with love.

The Bible says to forgive others just as Jesus has forgiven you. You will become more like Him by giving forgiveness to others. Pray and forgive!

Think About It
How can you forgive someone who has hurt you?

My Decrees

- I decree that I will keep bitterness out of my heart and not hold grudges.

- I decree that I will walk in love and forgiveness.

- I declare that I will keep a right attitude and not allow any anger or hurt to live in me.

- Thank You for helping me to forgive others as You have forgiven me.

MY BROKEN FAMILY

"The Lord your God goes with you; he will never leave you nor forsake you."
(Deuteronomy 31:6 NIV)

Family was God's idea from the beginning of creation. God gave rules for the husband, wife, and children. When those rules are followed, the family unit is strong, loving, and happy. But sometimes the rules are broken and the family becomes sad and troubled. Every circumstance is different but know you are not responsible for your family's actions.

What can you do if your family is hurting or broken? The most important thing you can do is continue your relationship with Jesus. Don't allow your hurt and sadness to cause you to pull away from God; now is a time to draw even closer. Talk to God about your feelings. He already knows your thoughts so He can handle whatever you need to say! Remember, you have a heavenly Father who loves you and will never leave or forsake you.

Think About It
How can God help you and your family?

My Decrees

- I decree that You are faithful to watch over my family during troubled times.

- I declare that that You are more than enough to handle my feelings.

- I declare that nothing can separate me from Your love.

- I declare that I will draw closer to You through hard times; I will not pull away.

- Thank You for never leaving me.

23 LYING

"Don't lie to each other, for you have stripped off your old sinful nature and all its wicked deeds."
(Colossians 3:9 NLT)

You should never lie. You should always tell the truth. The Bible says that God never lies. He is always honest. To be more like Jesus, you should also be truthful.

Sometimes it's hard, though! For instance, if you break something and you think you're going to get in trouble, you may be tempted to lie about it. However, if you lie, your parents will lose their trust in you. You need to be truthful because you want people to believe you.

Also, as a Christian, you have a beautiful truth to share with the world: the truth that Jesus loves them. If you are known as a liar, they may not believe you about Jesus even though what you say is true!

Lying can hurt others and it can hurt you. Being honest is a very important part of your character. Make the choice to tell the truth, no matter what.

Think About It
Why is being honest important?

My Decrees

- I decree that I will speak truth!

- I declare that I will be known as an honest person, not as a liar.

- I declare that because You live in me, I am able to overcome any temptation to lie.

- God never lies and neither will I.

- Thank You for being my Helper.

24

KEEP MAKING MISTAKES

*"For all have sinned and fall
short of the glory of God."*
(Romans 3:23 NIV)

What do you do if you're writing with a pencil and you make a mistake? You erase it and start over. Sometimes in life you're going to make mistakes. You might make a bad choice or say the wrong thing. God is not looking for perfection from you; He just wants your willing heart. He might be displeased at times about your choices but He will never give up on you. God's love for you will never change.

Many people in the Bible made mistakes. Peter denied he knew Jesus out of fear, Abraham lied, David blew it many times, but God still used each of them in great ways! If you make a mistake, ask God to forgive you and keep going. Being a Christian is a lifelong journey and He will help you every step of the way. God will erase your mistakes and use you, just as He used the great men and women of the Bible!

My Decrees

- I decree that even when I fail or make a mistake, I will get right back up and do better.

- I declare Your promise—if I sin, I can come to You and ask forgiveness and You are faithful to forgive.

- I declare that You are working in me and helping me to learn and grow up in Your ways.

- Thank You for never giving up on me.

25 ADDICTIVE HABITS

"I can do all this through him
who gives me strength."
(Philippians 4:13 NIV)

S ometimes you may feel a little overwhelmed and you want to do something to escape the busyness of life. You might enjoy playing video games, exercising, watching a show, or being on your phone. These can all be great things to enjoy. Did you know someone your age spends an average of six to nine hours a day looking at a screen?[2] That's like a whole day at school!

Do you sometimes find it hard to stop playing a video game or checking your phone? An addictive habit is when you have the inability to stop doing something on your own. Playing a video game is not bad, but it is if you don't get your homework done because of it. Then it becomes something that is controlling you and your actions.

At your age you are developing patterns that will go with you into adulthood. If you can set boundaries on your time now it will help you later in life. Ask God to help you with any addictive habits you may have. He will give you the strength to overcome because He cares so much about you!

My Decrees

- I decree that there is nothing too hard for You and I can be free from any addictive habits that are not good for me.

- I declare that I will not be a time waster.

- I decree that I will set and keep my priorities straight.

- Thank You for giving me the strength to overcome.

TEMPTATION

"The temptations in your life are no different from what others experience. And God is faithful. He will not allow the temptation to be more than you can stand. When you are tempted, he will show you a way out so that you can endure."
(1 Corinthians 10:13 NLT)

Temptation is the desire to do or want something that you know you shouldn't. Temptation can range from wanting an extra cookie to lying, cheating, or stealing. Did you know even Jesus faced temptation?

In the book of Mark, we read about a time when Jesus fasted, meaning he did not eat for 40 days. That is a long time to go without food! Can you imagine how hungry He must have been? Satan knew Jesus would be very hungry so he tried to tempt Jesus to eat. Jesus responded by quoting Scripture, the words of God, to help him resist temptation. The Bible says satan tried two other times to tempt Jesus and both times Jesus used Scripture to help him avoid temptation.

God promises that when you are tempted He will provide a way out. You don't have to give in to temptation. Jesus did the right thing and you can too!

My Decrees

- I decree that You live in me and You are greater than any temptation I face.

- I declare that I am an overcomer because You are my help in time of need.

- I declare that when I'm tempted to do the wrong thing I can defeat the enemy with Your Word.

- Thank You for making a way for me to do the right thing.

27 DOUBT

"Then Jesus told him, 'You believe because you have seen me. Blessed are those who believe without seeing me'"
(John 20:29 NLT)

In the book of John there is a story about a man named Thomas. Thomas had been a disciple of Jesus for three years when Jesus was crucified and rose back to life. After Jesus rose from the dead He appeared to all His disciples, except for Thomas who wasn't with them. The disciples told Thomas about Jesus but Thomas had a hard time believing something he could not see.

Thomas is often referred to as "Doubting Thomas." He doubted the resurrection was true because he didn't see it. However, all that changed when Thomas finally saw Jesus. His doubt transformed to faith the minute he saw Jesus.

Everyone has doubts sometimes. God does not get upset if you doubt Him, He uses it as an opportunity to grow your faith. Jesus promised that when you seek Him with all your heart you will find Him (see Jeremiah 29:13). Don't allow doubt to stop you from seeking God. He will be there to give you faith!

My Decrees

- I decree that I will believe You no matter what I see or don't see.

- I declare that I will not give in just because I don't see or understand completely.

- I decree that I will not doubt. I will trust what You say.

- Thank You for coming to me in times of doubt and growing my faith.

28 BROKEN-HEARTED

"The Lord is close to the brokenhearted; he rescues those whose spirits are crushed."
(Psalm 34:18 NLT)

God knows there will be hard moments in your life. A loved one may die, someone in your family might get a divorce, or someone close to you may experience an ongoing sickness. There may also be times when you feel brokenhearted over situations in the world. Sometimes it can be scary to listen to things on the news, and other times things you hear about may cause you to feel very sad.

The verse above from Psalm 34 tells you that God will be close to you during difficult times. When you are at your lowest moment, God steps in to be near. If you are brokenhearted, He will help heal you and put you together again. If your soul feels crushed, He will lift you up. God is always available to help you. You are not alone. God is with you and He loves you.

Think About It
How can God help your broken heart?

My Decrees

- I decree that You are with me always, through good times and bad, and nothing can separate me from Your love.

- I declare that Your joy and peace will flood my life and heal me when my heart is sad or troubled.

- I declare that You fill every empty place in me. You rescue and restore me.

- Thank You for healing me when my heart is broken.

NEEDING DIRECTION/ GUIDANCE

"Your word is a lamp to guide my
feet and a light for my path."
(Psalm 119:105 NLT)

Imagine you needed to go outside because you left your shoes in the backyard and the sun had already set. Then it was really dark. Most likely you would get a flashlight to help you see. When you turned the light on you could see the path to your shoes. As long as you kept the light on you could get your shoes and return safely back to your house.

The Bible is your light in the darkness. It is God's very Word. By reading and memorizing the Bible you can keep this flashlight with you at all times. If you are not sure which direction to take in life, there are Scriptures that will light up the way for you. Reading the Bible is a light for your life's path and its words help you know the things God wants for you. When you walk with God you walk with confidence.

Think About It

How can you use God's Word like a light?

My Decrees

- I decree that when it is the darkest or the hardest to understand, Your light shines brighter and makes my path clear.

- I declare that I will hear Your voice, even through Your Word, and nothing can hold me back.

- I declare that Your light is brighter than anything else in my life.

- Thank You that Your Word is a flashlight that lights my path.

30 FEEL DISCONNECTED FROM GOD

"Come close to God, and God will come close to you."
(James 4:8 NLT)

Have you ever done a water balloon toss? You begin by facing a partner a couple of feet apart and toss the balloon to each other. If you catch it, then each of you take a step back. The farther apart you become, the harder it is to catch the balloon. It is the same way with God. The farther away you are from Him, the harder it is to have a relationship with Him.

If you are feeling disconnected from God, you can take steps to be closer. You get closer to God by reading your Bible, praying, attending church, and spending time in worship. The closer you stay with God, the easier it will be to go through life. He will help you stay on the right path to fulfill your purpose as you grow closer in your relationship with Him.

Think About It
How will being close to Jesus help you?

My Decrees

- I decree that nothing will keep me from a close relationship with You.

- I declare that I will be strong and do great things by keeping You first in my life.

- I decree that I will walk toward You, not away from You.

- Thank You that as I get closer to You, You come closer to me.

NOTES

1. "Stomachaches," *Nemours KidsHealth*, reviewed by Elana Pearl Ben-Joseph, MD, February 2019, https://kidshealth.org/en/parents/stomachaches.html/.

2. "Screen Time vs. Lean Time Infographic," Division of Nutrition, Physical, Activity, and Obesity, CDC, https://www.cdc.gov/nccdphp/dnpao/multimedia/infographics/getmoving.html/.

STEP INTO PURPOSE

(Ages 0–6th Grade)

1 PURPOSE

*"You can make many plans, but the
Lord's purpose will prevail."*
(Proverbs 19:21 NLT)

Purpose is the reason why something exists. For example, a fire is built to keep you warm. A piano is played to make music. An oven is used to cook food. God also created *you* with a specific purpose. You were uniquely made with very special talents and gifts that the world needs. You may love to draw, so perhaps you'll become an artist or an architect. You might enjoy math, science, reading, or writing. Perhaps your gift is that you are an incredible friend or a strong athlete. The gifts you have are like road signs to where God is directing you.

You will find your purpose by knowing, loving, and serving God. You may not know much about your future, but you can be confident that God promises amazing blessings and that He has a plan for you that was determined long before you were even born!

Think About It

What skills, talents, and character qualities has God given you?

My Decrees

- I decree that God's plan and purpose for my life will be revealed as I serve Him, using the talents and gifts He has placed in me.

- I decree that God is revealing things to me that He planned before I was ever born.

- I decree that He made me with everything I need to accomplish His purpose.

- Thank You for providing special plans for my life.

2 IDENTITY

*"I will praise You, for I am fearfully
and wonderfully made."*
(Psalm 139:14 NKJV)

Identity is who you are. As a Christian, your identity is known through your relationship with Jesus. The Bible says you are *"fearfully and wonderfully made."* God created billions of people in this world, yet gave each one his or her own look, talent, strength, and personality.

As a younger person, your story is still being written. Part of who you are is based on things that will happen to you. As one who believes in Jesus, trust that He is helping to write your story. Place the pen in His hands and see the amazing things He has planned for you.

You were uniquely made in the image of God. Have you ever tried to look at your own face? The only way to view your face is to look in a mirror and see its reflection. This is called an image. When God made you, you were made as a reflection of Himself, which means you are made like Him! You were made to reflect the image of God. You are special to Him and He loves you!

Think About It
**What are some of the wonderful ways
in which God created you?**

My Decrees

- I decree that I am a child of God designed in His image and made for His glory.

- I decree that God is writing my story.

- I decree that I am exactly who God made me to be. I am a reflection of Him.

- I'm thankful that Your wisdom has planned me well.

3 DESTINY

*"Before I shaped you in the womb, I knew
all about you. Before you saw the light
of day, I had holy plans for you."*
(Jeremiah 1:5 MSG)

You are valuable and very important to God. Before there was even one day to your life, God thought about you and created a purpose and plan for you to complete. He took time to think about you and the Bible says He wrote amazing ideas for you before you were even born!

Remember, He created you with special skills, talents, and abilities, but you have a choice about what you do with your gifts. As you pray, listen to and obey God, He will help guide you in completing the plans He made for you. As you use the special gifts He gave you for His glory you are fulfilling your destiny, which is God's unique special plan for your life. For His glory simply means living in such a way that it points others to Jesus. The more you become like Jesus, the more you will see your destiny fulfilled.

God has awesome plans for you. Your destiny is good and your future is bright!

My Decrees

- I decree that before I was born God placed in me everything I would need to accomplish my destiny.

- I decree that I will use the special skills, talents, and abilities God has given me.

- I decree that I will pray, listen, and obey God so that the plans He made for my life will be completed.

- Thank You for the holy plans You made for my life.

4 POTENTIAL

"God can do anything, you know—far more than you could ever imagine or guess or request in your wildest dreams! He does it not by pushing us around but by working within us, his Spirit deeply and gently within us."
(Ephesians 3:20-21 MSG)

Potential is a certain ability that can be developed into a skill in the future. For example, professional athletes are not born professional athletes. They have a schedule they follow and it includes a lot of practice. Anyone who becomes excellent at a certain skill has put in a lot of time and effort. When athletes have reached their potential, their skill has fully developed.

The opposite can also be said. If a person, for example, only practices the piano sometimes, they might be okay at it but not as good as they could be. This means they have not reached their potential.

God wants you to reach your potential. He gave you gifts, talents, and skills for a reason—to use them! Set a goal and begin working on becoming better at the gifts God has given you.

Think About It

**What is a goal you can set for yourself
to help you reach your potential?**

My Decrees

- I decree that I will not waste my potential.

- I decree that I will set goals that please Him to fulfill dreams He places in my heart.

- I decree that all things are possible with God and He always does far more than I can ask or think.

- Thank You that my potential is awesome!

5 CHOSEN

*"Even before he made the world, God loved us
and chose us in Christ to be holy and without
fault in his eyes. God decided in advance to
adopt us into his own family by bringing us to
himself through Jesus Christ. This is what he
wanted to do, and it gave him great pleasure."*
(Ephesians 1:4-5 NLT)

It is amazing to think God chose you for a special blessing before He even made the world! He considers you special and set apart. Our opening verses also say that He has adopted you. Adoption means that someone chooses to take a child as their own, a child not born to them biologically. Bringing a child into a family is a meaningful and special life-changing decision.

Being in a family should mean having unconditional love without working to earn it. Typically, parents give their children what they need simply because they are part of the family. You are also God's child and He gives you what you need because He loves you and has from the very beginning. He calls you His own and has a special plan for you.

My Decrees

- I decree that God loves me, He chose me, and He wanted me in His family.

- I decree that He believes I am special and He takes care of all my needs.

- I declare that I belong to Him and He will never leave me.

- Thank You that I am a child of God and that You love me unconditionally.

6 FUTURE

"'For I know the plans I have for you,' says the Lord. 'They are plans for good and not for disaster, to give you a future and a hope.'"
(Jeremiah 29:11 NLT)

Builders can't build a house without having a plan. They also must make sure everything is measured correctly. If you have one wall that is too short the whole thing could fall down. If you forget to add a door no one can get in! Having a plan is important.

Your life is like a beautiful house and God is the Builder. He says in the book of Jeremiah that He has good plans for you. God wants to lead you in His perfect plan for your life. The future can sometimes seem scary because there are so many unknowns, but God holds your days in His very capable hands. You may not know how your destiny is going to unfold, but He does. You can look forward to your future knowing that God wants wonderful things for you. Believe God loves you and you will have a hope-filled future!

Think About It

What are some good plans you think God has for you?

My Decrees

- I decree that God's plan for my life is good and filled with hope! He has my future in His hands.

- I declare that as I follow Him, He will reveal His plans more and more and this gives me peace.

- I decree that I will not fear for He is with me and He is for me.

- Thank You that my future is in Your hands.

7 FRIENDSHIPS

"The righteous choose their friends carefully."
(Proverbs 12:26 NIV)

Friendships are an important part of our lives. You need friends but you also need to have the right friends. The Bible says a true friend should show love at all times. A true friend is also loyal and helps you when you need it.

Real friends bring out the best in each other. Your friends' attitudes and personalities rub off on you. Little by little, you become more and more like the people who surround you. If you surround yourself with negative people then they'll have a negative impact on your life. That's why it's so important to surround yourself with positive people. Pray that God would bless you with good friends that will encourage, love, and support you. Also know the greatest friend you could ever have is Jesus and He is happy to call you friend.

Think About It

**Why is it so important to
choose our friends carefully?**

My Decrees

- I decree that Jesus is my best friend and He will never leave me.

- I declare that I will make good and wise choices for friends
  and I will be a good friend to others.

- I declare that I will be a loyal friend.

- Thank You for my friends.

8 WORSHIP

"You are worthy, O Lord our God, to receive glory and honor and power. For you created all things, and they exist because you created what you pleased."
(Revelation 4:11 NLT)

Has your dad, mom, or a family member ever done something really special for you, and all you wanted to do was give them a big hug? Or maybe your parents got you a gift you really wanted for your birthday, or made you your favorite meal? Did that make you excited or happy on the inside?

God is your spiritual Father and when you worship God, it is a response to all the good things He has done for you. God loves you, protects you, gives you strength when you're weak, and so much more. You can't physically give God a hug but you can worship Him.

Worship is simply spending time with God. This can include singing, dancing, praying, or thinking about Him. It's a way to focus on God and who He is. As you worship your heart begins to respond to the wonder and greatness of God.

My Decrees

- I decree that I will worship God because of who He is.

- I decree that I will worship Him because He deserves thanks and praise for all He has done and is doing in my life.

- I declare that I will put Him first because He is worthy and I want to spend time with Him.

- Thank You for being my good, good Father.

9 WITNESS

"But you will receive power when the Holy Spirit comes upon you. And you will be my witnesses, telling people about me everywhere—in Jerusalem, throughout Judea, in Samaria, and to the ends of the earth."
(Acts 1:8 NLT)

A witness is someone who saw, knew, or experienced something. As we see in our opening verse, Jesus told His disciples, *"Be my witnesses, telling people about me everywhere. . . ."* Being a witness for Jesus means talking about the things you know to be true about Him.

There are many ways to be a witness for Jesus. You can talk about the things you have experienced. Being a witness also means reflecting His image by showing His characteristics. For example, if someone is feeling bad, guilty, or embarrassed about something they have done, you are Jesus's witness when you show kindness to them. You could also tell about God's forgiveness, you can encourage people, you can share important truths you know about Him, and you can pray for them. Use your life to help point others to Jesus.

Think About It

**What are some other ways
you can be a witness for Jesus?**

My Decrees

- I decree that Holy Spirit will help me be a strong witness to others about Jesus.

- I declare that I will tell others how Jesus can help them and make a difference in their lives.

- I declare that I will do my best to represent Him well by being truthful, kind, forgiving, and loving.

- Thank You for giving me opportunities to share Your love with others.

10 COURAGE

*"This is my command—be strong and courageous!
Do not be afraid or discouraged. For the Lord
your God is with you wherever you go."*
(Joshua 1:9 NLT)

C*ourage* is another word for *being brave*. Courage means doing something even if you are afraid.

Our Bible verse says, *"For the Lord your God is with you wherever you go."* This means that being strong and courageous is not based on your ability but on God's. For example, suppose you were riding your bike and a dog came at you out of nowhere. You start to feel scared but then remember that your dad is riding bikes with you. A feeling of strength and courage comes over you, not because you were suddenly bigger and stronger, but because of the strength and courage of your dad and you trusted in that. That's the kind of *"strong and courageous"* this verse is talking about. This kind of courage is based on something stronger than us, which is God.

Instead of worrying about how big your fear is, be courageous, and remember how big Your God is!

Think About It
In what area of life do you feel you need some strength or courage?

My Decrees

- I decree that because God is with me wherever I go I am brave and strong and can do hard things.

- I do not have to be afraid or upset because I am never alone.

- I decree that fear has no place in my life because God is bigger!

- Thank You that nothing is too hard for You.

11 WISDOM

"For the Lord gives wisdom; from His mouth come knowledge and understanding."
(Proverbs 2:6 NKJV)

Wisdom is knowing what is right and doing it. For example, you are wise when you know the rules at home or at school and you choose to obey them. You are also wise when you read the Bible and follow its commands.

A great example of wisdom from the Bible is found in the story of Solomon. When Solomon was set to become the next king of Israel, God came to him in a dream and offered to grant him a request, anything that he wanted! I bet Solomon had to think hard about this, but he came up with a great reply. He knew that if he was to lead the people as God's servant, he would need to know how to choose right from wrong. He would need to make a lot of important decisions for the people and rule them well, so Solomon asked the Lord for wisdom and understanding.

True wisdom comes when you ask God for it and He is happy to give it to you. When you pray, listen to God, and study His Word, you will know the right choices to make.

My Decrees

- I decree that I will ask God for wisdom to make right choices.

- I declare that I will stay in God's Word and live my life the way He teaches me, and I will follow His commands.

- I declare that I will not be foolish. I will be wise and make smart decisions.

- Thank You that when I ask for wisdom You always give it to me.

12 FEAR OF THE LORD

"'For I am a great king,' says the Lord Almighty,
'and my name is to be feared among the nations.'"
(Malachi 1:14 NIV)

I t may seem strange to talk about fearing the Lord. Isn't He loving, kind, and good? Yes, He is all of these things! Fearing the Lord doesn't mean being afraid of Him. It means to respect and honor Him.

To fear the Lord you must know who He is. The more you know who God is, the greater you will love Him and want to show Him respect. You can think about this in relation to your friends. You're probably not afraid of your friends, but when you make some decisions you might be concerned what your friends might think. That is how you should be with God.

Anytime you are making a decision or are about to do something, you should think, *What will God think about this? Will this make Him happy?* You should care a lot more about what God thinks than what your friends think. That doesn't mean you should be afraid of God; it just means you want to live for Him.

God is good. God is love. God is kind and He wants what is best for you and your life.

Think About It
Is God scary?
What does it mean to fear the Lord?

My Decrees

- I decree that I will respect the Lord at all times.

- I declare that I will always honor Him.

- I declare that God is my Friend and I have nothing to fear.

- Thank You, God, for wanting what is best for me.

13 KNOWLEDGE

"The people who know their God shall be strong."
(Daniel 11:32 NKJV)

You can have knowledge in your life about many things, such as science, history, football, music, or video games. However, knowing God is the best knowledge you will ever have! The best way to get to know God is to spend time with Him. You can do this by reading the Bible, praying, or worshipping Him. As you do these things your knowledge of God grows and your faith is strengthened.

We all have attributes, which are ways to describe ourselves: fast, tall, short, a twin, athletic, creative, kind, and so on. But when we talk about God, He has attributes that belong *only* to Him. They are the things that make Him God. Knowing the truth of who God is will help you stand strong in your faith.

Think About It

How can you know God more?
What are some of God's attributes?

My Decrees

- I decree that I will run after God with all I've got in order to know Him and His ways.

- I decree that the more I know Him, the more I have understanding of who He is and how that helps me to grow as a Christian.

- I decree that I will pray, read His Word, and spend time with Him.

- Thank You that knowing You makes me strong.

14 OBEDIENCE

"He replied, 'Blessed rather are those who hear the word of God and obey it.'"
(Luke 11:28 NIV)

P art of living the purpose God has for your life includes building your character, and obedience is one thing that builds character.

The Bible is your road map in life and many verses speak about the importance of obedience. Obedience is when you do what you are told by your parents, a trusted adult, or God. Rules are made for your protection. For example, what would happen if cars didn't stop at a red light? There would be a lot of accidents! Or what if you were allowed to stay up very late every night? Your body wouldn't be as healthy or grow the way it should because you need sleep.

Rules that need to be obeyed can sometimes seem hard or opposite of what you want to do, but they are set by God and your family to help you have a fulfilled life. Disobeying can cause hurt and pain, but obeying helps your life go more smoothly.

Jesus said in John 14:21 (NLT), *"Those who accept my commandments and obey them are the ones who love me."* One of the ways you can show your love to God is by choosing to obey each and every day.

My Decrees

- I decree that I will learn to trust and obey God because His Word is for my good.

- I declare that I will follow His commandments.

- I decree that I will do what God tells me to do.

- I thank You that I am blessed because I hear Your Word and obey it.

15 PERSEVERANCE

"And let us run with perseverance
the race marked out for us."
(Hebrews 12:1 NIV)

Have you ever signed up to play a sport, but halfway through wanted to quit? Or maybe it was piano lessons or art classes that you didn't want to do anymore. Chances are, if this has happened to you, your parents probably said something like, "You started it; you finish it." Perseverance is continuing to do something even if it's hard. It means not giving up.

Many things God asks you to do aren't easy—like saying no to temptation, being nice to those who aren't nice to you, or even sharing about Him with others. The good thing is you don't have to persevere on your own. God loves to help you! He wants to encourage you to keep going and not give up. Put your trust in God and allow Him to help you do what's right.

Life may not always be easy, but with God by your side you can persevere and it can be awesome!

Think About It
Why is it important to persevere?

My Decrees

- I decree that with God's help, I will not give up, give in, or back down from persevering.

- I decree that I will always give my best and if I mess up He will help me up and we will keep going!

- I decree that with God I can do all things and that includes the hard things.

- Thank You for helping me to always keep going and never give up.

16 SERVING

"For even the Son of Man came not to be served but to serve others and to give his life as a ransom for many."
(Matthew 20:28 NLT)

Have you ever been asked to help a friend, parent, or teacher and the first thing you thought was, *What's in it for me?* For example, your mom asks you to wash the dishes or take out the trash and you wonder if you will get paid. Or your dad asks you to help clean up the yard and you hope that means you'll get a new video game. It's as if the only reason you want to help is because you may get something out of it. Serving others is the opposite of that thought process. Serving is not about what people can do for you; it's about what you can do for them. It doesn't require any special gift or talent; it's simply giving to others.

Jesus said if you want to be great, learn to serve. It could be holding the door open for someone who has their hands full or helping clean up a mess that you didn't make. Jesus showed the importance of serving others when He came to earth. In fact, it's the whole reason He came! You should serve others because you love and serve God.

My Decrees

- I decree that I will serve as if I am doing it for the Lord, because I am.

- I declare that I will serve others expecting nothing in return.

- I declare that I will joyfully serve.

- Thank You for showing me how to serve.

17 CONSISTENCY

"Whatever is good and perfect is a gift coming down to us from God our Father, who created all the lights in the heavens. He never changes or casts a shifting shadow."
(James 1:17 NLT)

What does a shifting shadow mean? As the sun changes position in the sky, its light hits objects from different angles and causes the shadows to look differently. Our opening Bible verse assures us that God never changes. He is always the same, unlike shadows. Isn't that encouraging?

The consistency of God is important because it means He is always someone you can depend on and trust. Because God is consistent and the goal is to be more like Him, it is important for you to be consistent too. You can be consistent with God, others, and your behavior. Some ideas of being consistent with God would be praying, reading your Bible, and going to church. With others you can be caring, friendly and happy to help when needed. You can also be consistent with your attitude and personality. How wonderful it is to know God never changes and you can always trust Him!

Think About It

How can you be consistent in your life?

My Decrees

- I decree that I will allow God to work in me and help me to develop consistency in my life in the ways I serve Him.

- I decree that I will work on being consistent with my behavior.

- I decree that I will make any changes in my life necessary to help me achieve this.

- Thank You, God, that You are always the same.

18 THANKFULNESS

"Always be joyful. Never stop praying. Be thankful in all circumstances, for this is God's will for you who belong to Christ Jesus."
(1 Thessalonians 5:16-18 NLT)

Have you ever received a gift from someone and your mom had to remind you to say thank you? Saying thank you is a way to recognize and show appreciation to someone who has done something for you.

There is a story in the Bible about ten men who went to Jesus, hoping to be healed. All of them walked away with their healing, but only one came back to praise and thank Jesus for it. I guess their moms weren't there to remind them!

It is important to express thanks to God in all things, even when you may be having a bad day. For example, I know a family whose home was flooded because of a bad storm. All of their furniture was ruined and they lost a lot of valuable items. Yet this family was still thankful to God that they weren't harmed and they praised Him for that. Part of God's plan and hope for your life is that you would choose to see the good, even if things are going wrong. Choose to be thankful and give God praise.

Think About It

**What are some things you
can thank God for in your life?**

My Decrees

- I decree that I will practice being thankful, grateful every day for the small things and the big things that God does in my life.

- I declare that I will practice this with my family and friends as well.

- I decree that giving thanks will become a part of who I am.

- Thank You, Jesus, for every thing! You deserve all the praise.

HUMILITY

"He guides the humble in what is right and teaches them his way."
(Psalm 25:9 NIV)

Humility is the ability to consider others ahead of yourself. It is being confident without thinking you are better than everyone else.

God created you with special talents, gifts, and abilities and He created others with special strengths too. Some examples of being humble are speaking well of others, congratulating someone for a job well done, avoiding bragging, being patient with others, and apologizing when you've made a mistake. When a person is willing to admit they have sinned and are sorry, God is pleased with their attitude. However, God is not pleased when a person points out someone else's faults or brags about themselves without seeing their own flaws.

You should definitely be proud of your talents and gifts while still acknowledging they came from God. When you don't act like you can do it all on your own, that is when God can work through you. He is pleased when your heart is humble.

My Decrees

- I declare that I will not think or act like I am better than anyone else.

- I declare that I will speak well of others.

- I declare that I will apologize when I've made a mistake.

- I decree that I will remember that every good gift comes from God and will always give Him the glory.

- Thank You that when I'm humble before You, You will guide and teach me Your way.

20 Reading the Bible

"I have hidden your word in my heart,
that I might not sin against you."
(Psalm 119:11 NLT)

Reading the Bible is one of the most important things you can do. The Bible is God's Word, and all Scripture is "God-breathed." That means it's all from God and it's all useful and true. The Bible tells you so much about God—who He is and what He's like. It also gives you important instructions for how to live your life. In fact, you could spend your whole life reading the Bible and still learn something new every time you pick it up!

You may have questions as you are reading parts of the Bible, and it's important to ask a trusted adult to help answer them. Sometimes you may read a section that you don't agree with. You don't read the Bible to tell you what you want to hear though, you read it to know what is true.

One of the best things you can do with Scripture is memorize it. When you hide God's Word in your heart it will always be there for when you need it most. Pick up your Bible. Read it, learn it, and live it!

Think About It
Why is it important to read your Bible?

My Decrees

- I decree that I will read God's Word and ask Him to help me apply it to my life.

- I decree that I will study and memorize God's Word.

- I declare that God's Word will work in me and through me.

- Thank You, God, for Your Word that breathes life into me.

21
NOT TOO YOUNG

"'O Sovereign Lord,' I said, 'I can't speak for you! I'm too young!' The Lord replied, 'Don't say, "I'm too young," for you must go wherever I send you and say whatever I tell you.'"
(Jeremiah 1:6-7 NLT)

Have you ever experienced not being able to do something because you were too young or too small? I remember I couldn't wait to be tall enough to ride big roller coasters! Sometimes we think we have to wait to be old enough to do things for God, but He wants to use us at any age.

In the Bible, God came to someone named Jeremiah and told him that he was going to be a prophet. That means God was giving Jeremiah the special job of telling people the words that God was saying. Jeremiah wondered how he could do something so important since he was so young. God promised to be with Jeremiah and to give him the courage and strength he needed.

As you read your Bible and pray, God will show you things He wants you to do too. It may be something as simple as sitting by someone new or telling someone how much God loves them. You don't have to wait until you're older to do great things for God. He wants to use you right now!

Think About It
In what ways can God use you right now?

My Decrees

- I decree that my young age will not stop me from learning and serving the Lord, no matter what anyone says.

- I decree that I will keep growing up in Him by reading His Word and using the gifts He has put inside me to help others.

- I decree that I will keep at it, doing and saying what God says.

- Thank You that my age doesn't matter to You. You will use me.

TRAINING YOUR THOUGHTS

"And now, dear brothers and sisters, one final thing. Fix your thoughts on what is true, and honorable, and right, and pure, and lovely, and admirable. Think about things that are excellent and worthy of praise."
(Philippians 4:8 NLT)

Your thoughts affect you much more than you may think. If you are thinking about something scary, you'll start to feel scared. If your mind is constantly worrying about something sad, you may start feeling depressed. What you think about you become.

The Bible says to *"fix your thoughts on what is true . . . and lovely."* *Lovely thoughts* simply means thinking on things that are good. Instead of thinking about problems that may leave you feeling stressed out, think on other things.

It is important to remember that Jesus loves you very much. God made you exactly the way He wanted and thinks you are very special. You can obey Him because God has given you the strength to follow His commands. By thinking on lovely thoughts, the bad thoughts get pushed away.

Train your thoughts to think on the truths from God's Word.

Think About It
**What are some good things God
wants you to think about?**

My Decrees

- I decree that I will think good things!

- I decree that I will be careful in what I watch, read, and listen to and in the games I play.

- I will replace bad thoughts with good thoughts.

- Thank You, Jesus, for helping me think the right things.

23
SPIRITUAL AUTHORITY

"I have given you authority to trample on snakes and scorpions and to overcome all the power of the enemy; nothing will harm you."
(Luke 10:19 NIV)

As a child of God you also have authority in Christ. It is your connection, relationship and dependence on Jesus that give you this authority. This means you have the right to use the power of God's Name when you pray.

Have you ever had a nightmare and ran to your parents' room for comfort? Perhaps they prayed with you and told the nightmares to leave. Did you know you can do that too? As a child of God, you can command nightmares to *go* in the Name of Jesus! The Name of Jesus is powerful because we are talking about the Person, Jesus Christ, His character, and the things He does. As believers we know there is power in His Name because of who He is. Trust that as you pray in His Name His power will be released in the situation.

Think About It
What are some things you
can pray about in Jesus's Name?

My Decrees

- I decree that I have the right to use the Name of Jesus to change things that are not from Him.

- I decree that satan has no power over me.

- I declare that angels are all around me and are protecting me.

- Thank You for the authority I have in Your Name.

DREAMING BIG

"God has given each of you a gift from his great variety of spiritual gifts. Use them well to serve one another."
(1 Peter 4:10 NLT)

Don't be afraid to do what God has called you to do. God has given you gifts and abilities and He wants you to use them!

In the parable of the talents, Jesus told a story about a master with three servants. To each of his servants he gave a number of talents. Today we use the word *talent* to mean something you are good at but in Bible days talent meant a lot of money, such as a big bag of gold. Two of the servants used their talents to make more money but one of them buried his because he was afraid. When the master returned he was very happy with the servants who had used what they were given, but he was very unhappy with the servant who had hid his away.

God doesn't want you to be afraid to use your gifts. God wants you to dream big and to use the gifts He's given you!

Think About It
What gifts has God given you
and how can you use them?

My Decrees

- I decree that I will use the gifts the Lord has given me.

- I decree that I will not hide my gifts.

- I declare that I will not waste God-given dreams and I will go for them!

- Thank You, Lord, for the gifts and dreams You have given me.

25 GUARDING YOUR HEART

"Guard your heart above all else, for it determines the course of your life."
(**Proverbs 4:23 NLT**)

Have you ever seen a piñata? A piñata is a container often made of cardboard that is decorated, filled with candy, and then broken as part of a celebration. What if the piñata were filled with soggy vegetables? Would that be as fun? Of course not!

What the piñata is filled with is pretty important. It is the same way with your heart. What your heart is filled with comes out in your words and actions. Guarding your heart simply means protecting it. Two important ways to protect your heart is controlling what you see and what you hear. If you are watching and hearing good things, then good is what will fill your heart.

It's so important to guard your heart because the Bible says it controls everything you do. Guarding your heart will help you fulfill the plan God has for your life.

Think About It
Why is it important to guard your heart?

My Decrees

- I decree that my heart belongs to You and I will choose to fill it with good things.

- I decree that I will guard my heart and protect it with Your Word.

- I declare that I will listen for Your voice to lead me and keep me on the right path.

- Thank You for helping me guard my heart.

CALLING

"Lead a life worthy of your calling, for you have been called by God."
(Ephesians 4:1 NLT)

Have you thought about what you want to do when you're older? You know God created you for a purpose and has great plans for you. He has also placed a calling on your life. A calling is an invitation by God to a certain area of work. You may think you have to be a pastor or a worship leader to do great things for God and His Kingdom but that's not true. You can shine for Jesus wherever you work!

Being called by God doesn't only mean working in a church. You might be called to be a teacher, a chef, a news reporter, a politician, or a lawyer. Whatever you are interested in is a good sign of what God has planned for your life. He created you with certain skills and interests so you can pursue them. As you continue following Jesus, He will lead you to your calling.

Think About It

**What are some things you enjoy doing?
Do you have some ideas of what you'd
like to do when you're older?**

My Decrees

- I decree that my future is in Your hands and You have it all planned out for me.

- I decree that I will trust You to make my calling clear to me and You go before me to prepare the way.

- I declare that I will serve You all the days of my life in whatever ways You place in my heart to bring glory to Your Name.

- Thank You, Jesus, for leading me to my calling.

27 ZEAL

*"And you must love the Lord your God with all
your heart, all your soul, and all your strength."*
(Deuteronomy 6:5 NLT)

Have you ever heard the word *zeal?* To have zeal means you are filled with passion and enthusiasm for something. It means you are full of excitement about your faith. That's the kind of life God calls all Christians to live.

Being zealous for God means you are committed to God's way of doing things, not your own, and you are eager to embrace all that God wants to do in your life. God isn't calling you to only serve him a little bit or only love Him sometimes; He wants you to fully live for Him every day and in every way.

Ways to show your zeal for God include reading the Bible, praying, and worshipping Him. Your zeal for God will help you fulfill your destiny. Love Him with all your heart, soul, mind, and strength!

Think About It

What are some ways you can show your zeal for God?

My Decrees

- I decree that I will be excited about serving God.

- I decree that I will be filled with zeal and on fire for You.

- I decree that I will love You with all my heart, soul, mind, and strength.

- Thank You, God, for helping me live fully for You.

28 PEACEMAKERS

"Blessed are the peacemakers, for they
will be called children of God."
(Matthew 5:9 NIV)

It takes courage to be a peacemaker. If someone pushes you, you might want to push them back. Or if you get called a bad name, you might want to call them a worse one. You may think by reacting in those ways it will make you a winner in the eyes of others. While it may impress some people, it definitely doesn't impress God. If you win a fight or an argument you might get praise from other people. They may say what you did was awesome. But wouldn't you rather have God think what you did was awesome?

Whether it is a physical fight or an argument, you have a choice to make the situation worse or better. Often the best option is to walk away. Now there may be situations where you have to stand up for yourself or someone else, but if you can avoid a fight, that is amazing. Anyone can fight but it takes true courage and strength to stay peaceful.

Think About It
What does it look like to be a peacemaker?

My Decrees

- I decree that I will walk in peace and do my best to represent Jesus in every situation.

- I decree that I will not stir up anger and I will guard the words that come out of my mouth.

- I declare that I will walk in God's strength and will ask Him for His help in anything that comes my way.

- Thank You, God, for Your peace.

THE POWER
OF PRAYER

*"The earnest prayer of a righteous person has
great power and produces wonderful results."*
(James 5:16 NLT)

Prayer is one of the most powerful tools you have as a child of God. He promises that He hears you when you pray and there is nothing too hard or too big for Him to handle. He also promises to answer your prayer. You may not always get the answer you are hoping for, but God loves you very much and wants what is best for you. He is Lord of all, and He has a plan for everything.

The Bible says that God will work everything for your good. So if something you are praying about isn't good yet, keep praying and stay confident that God is working things out. Pray with boldness, knowing He is listening. You are His child and He loves spending time with you!

Think About It
Why should you pray?

My Decrees

- I decree that You are faithful to honor Your Word and You never fail us.

- I declare that You hear my prayers and answer them.

- I decree that when I ask, I receive. You are more than enough to meet every need I have.

- Thank You for being a good Father who gives good gifts to His children.

LIVING
GOD'S WAY

"Stay on the path that the Lord your God
has commanded you to follow. Then you will
live long and prosperous lives in the land
you are about to enter and occupy."
(Deuteronomy 5:33 NLT)

O ne awesome reason you can trust the Bible is that it just works! If you live your life God's way, you will have a life He planned and created just for you. It doesn't mean that you won't have any pain or struggles, but it does mean that you will be prepared to handle anything that life throws at you.

No other religion can promise and deliver the peace, love, joy, and fulfillment that comes from a life lived in obedience to Jesus Christ. A life without God is empty and full of needless pain and problems. If you learn what God says in the Bible and commit yourself to His way of doing things, you will not be disappointed. Remember, you are incredibly special to God and He loves you very much!

Think About It
Why should you live God's way?

My Decrees

- I decree that I will live my life Your way.

- I decree that I will always look to You for everything I need.

- I declare that I will follow You all the days of my life and keep my eyes fixed on You.

- I thank You for Your love and Your faithfulness that keep me on the right path.

RECEIVE PROMISES

(Ages 0 – 6th Grade)

1 GOD NEVER LIES

"God is not a man, so he does not lie. He is not human, so he does not change his mind. Has he ever spoken and failed to act? Has he ever promised and not carried it through?"
(Numbers 23:19 NLT)

God has promised many things to those who believe in Him. All these promises can be found in the Bible. You can trust and believe His words will happen for you because God has *never* broken a promise! That may be hard to believe because your experience may be that people break their word sometimes. Our opening verse says God is not a man, so He does not lie and He doesn't change His mind.

Sometimes people switch their decisions, but God will always push through with what He has promised. Your part in seeing God's promises come to pass is to trust Him. Even if you don't see the promises come exactly when you want, trust that He knows the perfect time to give them to you. Keep your hope and faith in Him. Believe God will be true to His Word. He will never fail you!

Think About It

Why can you trust in God's promises?

My Decrees

- I decree that every promise You have made is unchangeable and You will never let me down.

- I decree that Your promises never fail. You always come through.

- I decree that God never lies!

- Thank You that You are true to Your Word.

2 HOLY SPIRIT

"For all who are led by the Spirit of God are children of God."
(Romans 8:14 NLT)

In the Bible, you see three clear Persons: the Father, the Son, and the Holy Spirit. This is known as the Trinity. Just like an egg has three parts—the shell, the white, and the yolk—one God has three Persons.

Holy Spirit is your Helper. When you give your heart to Jesus, He cleanses your heart and puts His Holy Spirit inside you. When you need help, you can listen for what He is saying in your heart. There is so much more to Holy Spirit than that, though! He wants to fill and refill you every day to give you exactly what you need to follow Jesus and produce good fruit in your life.

Additionally, Holy Spirit helps you feel better when you're sad and helps you to know God's love. He gives you the words to pray when you don't know what to say and helps you speak the truth. He also helps you understand the Bible and Jesus more. Holy Spirit is your great Helper!

My Decrees

- I decree that Holy Spirit, You are my Helper and my Comforter.

- I decree that You help me to pray when I don't even know what to say.

- I declare that Your power is in me to overcome and to be strong when I feel weak.

- Thank You for being my great Helper.

3 FRUIT OF THE SPIRIT

"But the Holy Spirit produces this kind of fruit in our lives: love, joy, peace, patience, kindness, goodness, faithfulness, gentleness, and self-control. There is no law against these things!"
(Galatians 5:22-23 NLT)

The fruit of the Spirit is a gift from God to believers to help them live in ways that please Him and show His love to others. Imagine that the fruit of the spirit is like a basket filled with different kinds of yummy fruit. Each fruit represents a different quality that comes from God. The more you eat the fruit, the better you will feel inside.

Just as your body needs food to grow and be healthy, your spirit needs spiritual food to grow strong in God. This spiritual food is the fruit of the Spirit. The fruit of the Spirit is important because it shows you are living for God. These are characteristics that God wants you to have in your life because they reflect who He is. When you allow the Holy Spirit to lead and guide you, these qualities will be a part of your life.

My Decrees

- I decree that the fruit of the Spirit is in me and is working in every area of my life.

- I decree that the fruit of the Spirit helps me to be who You have designed me to be.

- I choose to grow the fruit of the Spirit in my life today.

- Thank You for leading and guiding me in Your ways.

4 LOVE

"Love is patient and kind. Love is not jealous or boastful or proud or rude. It does not demand its own way. It is not irritable, and it keeps no record of being wronged. It does not rejoice about injustice but rejoices whenever the truth wins out. Love never gives up, never loses faith, is always hopeful, and endures through every circumstance."
(1 Corinthians 13:4-7 NLT)

Love is the first fruit of the Spirit listed in Galatians. The Bible has a lot to say about love, and 1 Corinthians 13 has great verses to study about it. As a Christian you should do your best to show God's love to others. In fact, God commanded us to love Him and others just as He has loved us. So love is not only a fruit of the Spirit but it is also a command from God.

God showed His great love for you by sending His Son, Jesus, to die on the Cross for your sins. You can show love for others by putting them first and thinking of them more than yourself. Before you can truly love others, you must know and love God. Some great ways to love God are learning more about Him through reading the Bible, spending time with Him in prayer, and worshipping Him. Love will be a fruit produced by Holy Spirit as you grow in your relationship with Jesus.

Think About It
How can you show God's love to others?

My Decrees

- I decree that I will walk in love today.

- I declare that I will trust in Your love.

- I decree that nothing can separate me from Your love.

- Thank You for showing Your great love for me.

5 JOY

"I have told you this, so that my joy may be in you and that your joy may be complete."
(John 15:11 NIV)

If you are filled with Holy Spirit, then you are promised joy. Joy from God is different than being happy, so it is important to look in the Bible to see how His Word defines it.

In Psalm 119:111, the psalmist David said that God's Word was the joy of his heart. As you read the Bible you discover more about God, and your heart will be filled with joy. There is another verse in the Bible that says you should even consider it joy when you go through difficult times (see James 1:2). How can that be? Because joy is very different from happiness. You cannot be happy when you are sad, but you can have joy. Happiness is a feeling based on what is happening to you. Joy comes from knowing, believing, and trusting in God. When your joy comes from God, nothing can stop it!

Think About It

How is joy different from happiness?

My Decrees

- I decree that I have Your joy living in me and this joy is my strength.

- I choose to be joyful and this joy is found in You alone.

- I declare that You fill me and You have the best prepared for me. Even in hard times, this joy brings me peace.

- Thank You for filling my heart with joy.

6 PEACE

"And let the peace that comes from Christ rule in your hearts. For as members of one body you are called to live in peace. And always be thankful."
(Colossians 3:15 NLT)

What comes to your mind when you think of something peaceful? Maybe sitting on a comfy pillow while reading a book or being on a nice vacation? These things might give you peace for a time but it doesn't last.

Christians have God's peace, which is greater than anything the world can give. Peace is a fruit of the Spirit that only comes from God. Peace in God is knowing that He is always there for you, and that helps you feel safe and calm. The Bible says the peace of God will rule in your heart.

When you have God's peace you don't have to be worried and concerned about things. If you are anxious or stressed and need more peace in your life, try spending time with God. Let His Word and presence fill your heart. Live the way God leads you and you will find His true peace. There is nothing in the world that could ever compare to the biblical peace of God!

Think About It
What is God's peace?

My Decrees

- I decree that Your supernatural peace surrounds me.

- I declare that even if I don't fully understand, You are there for me, keeping me calm.

- I declare that stress and anxiety have no place in my life.

- I thank You for Your peace in my life.

7 PATIENCE

"Wait patiently for the Lord. Be brave and courageous. Yes, wait patiently for the Lord."
(Psalm 27:14 NLT)

You've probably heard your parents or an adult tell you to be patient. Patience can be really hard to have sometimes. There are so many things available to you so quickly that it can be difficult to wait when you there's no other option. You can go through a drive-through and have your favorite food in just minutes. You can place an online order and have it delivered in one day. You have streaming devices where you can watch whatever you want, whenever you want. So many things are very fast. But God still wants you to have patience.

Patience is a fruit of the Spirit; this means if you have Jesus then you can have patience. You might be thinking you can't be patient, but God says you can. It might be hard sometimes but nothing is impossible with God! Having patience will help you not to worry or stress when you are waiting on something. Ask God to help you and He will!

Think About It

Why is patience important?

My Decrees

- I decree that patience will have its perfect work in me.

- I decree that Your desire for my life cannot be held back and will arrive in Your perfect timing.

- I declare that You make all things beautiful at the right time.

- I declare that I will practice patience!

- Thank You for teaching me to be patient.

8 KINDNESS

"Be kind to one another, tenderhearted, forgiving one another, as God in Christ forgave you."
(Ephesians 4:32 ESV)

Being kind is a positive quality that God wants you to have. It is a fruit of the Spirit and God wants you to show kindness to everyone, even if they aren't kind to you. Kindness can be shown by your thoughts, actions, and words. No one is kind all the time, but the more you know God, the more you become like Him. God will give you the power to be kind and kindness will become part of your character.

Have you heard of random acts of kindness? Those are acts done for people without expecting anything in return. Some examples are holding the door for someone, giving a compliment, donating outgrown clothes, or writing positive chalk notes on your driveway. Try to do several kind things for people this week. This is a great way to grow the fruit of kindness in your life. Show the kindness to others that God has shown to you!

My Decrees

- I decree that because of You kindness is a way of life for me.

- I declare that You will give me creative ways to show kindness to others.

- I decree that I will walk in forgiveness and kindness to others so that I represent You well.

- Thank You for teaching me kindness.

9 GOODNESS

"So let's not get tired of doing what is good. At just the right time we will reap a harvest of blessing if we don't give up."
(Galatians 6:9 NLT)

Goodness is another fruit of the Spirit and you should be overflowing with it! With Holy Spirit living inside you He gives you the power to do good. This doesn't mean you will be good all the time. Everyone makes mistakes. But the closer you get to God, the more you will become like Him.

One of the most important beliefs of a Christian is that God is always good. God has promised His goodness to you. This means anything that happens in your life, good or bad, God will work it for good. This is such an important truth for you to know. If you are going through a tough time, remember the goodness of God.

You were also created to *do* good. Be compassionate and show God's goodness to others. The more you grow in your relationship with Jesus, the more this fruit will grow in your life. Before you know it, no one will need to tell you to be good; it will just be who you are!

Think About It

How can God's goodness be seen in your life?

My Decrees

- I decree that You are very good to me.

- I decree that I will reflect Your goodness to others. I just won't be able to help it!

- I declare that Your goodness runs after me, chases me down, and operates in my life.

- I declare that I will never give up or get tired of doing good.

- Thank You for teaching me goodness.

10 FAITHFULNESS

"But be sure to fear the Lord and faithfully serve him. Think of all the wonderful things he has done for you."
(1 Samuel 12:24 NLT)

The Bible tells us that God abounds in faithfulness. This means it overflows from Him. Faithful means staying true or loyal to someone. Faithfulness is a fruit of the Spirit so that means you can be faithful too.

The Bible has many verses instructing us to be faithful to God. You can be faithful by reading, knowing, and obeying His Word. You can also show faithfulness to God by praying to Him and worshipping Him. Spending time in God's presence helps you keep your eyes and thoughts on Him. There is nothing you can do that will stop His faithfulness. God will always be faithful to you. No matter what you do, He will always keep His Word and His promises will never be broken.

If you make a mistake, simply ask for forgiveness and keep doing your best to live for Him. Pray for faithfulness to grow and overflow in your heart.

My Decrees

- I decree that You are my God and You are faithful to provide for my every need.

- I declare my faithfulness to You and Your Word and I will not be influenced by any other.

- I decree that I will be found faithful and true and serve you all the days of my life.

- I decree that great is Your faithfulness!

- Thank You for teaching me about Your faithfulness.

11 GENTLENESS

"Let your gentleness be evident to all. The Lord is near."
(Philippians 4:5 NIV)

Have you ever been around a newborn baby and someone reminded you to be gentle? You're supposed to be careful with babies because if you are too rough, you could hurt them.

Gentleness is a fruit of the Spirit that God wants you to grow in your life. God wants you to be gentle in your words, actions, and attitudes. When you are gentle, you are showing that you care about someone or something. The Bible also says to be gentle in the way you talk with someone. When you are gentle with your words, you are showing you care about the person's feelings. Being gentle with someone else's property is another way to show you care. Jesus models gentleness to you by giving you comfort, peace, and love, and showing kindness and goodness to you. Ask God to grow the fruit of gentleness in your heart and to show you ways you can practice being gentle.

Think About It

How can I show gentleness to others?

My Decrees

- I decree that I will be gentle and kind—on purpose!

- I decree that I will say and do what is right in Your eyes.

- I decree that I will practice releasing the gentleness to all I encounter, including my family.

- I declare that I will watch my words and actions so that people see Jesus in me.

- Thank You for teaching me gentleness.

SELF-CONTROL

*"A person without self-control is like
a city with broken-down walls."*
(Proverbs 25:28 NLT)

Self-control is being in charge of your words, thoughts, feelings, and actions. It's obeying right away to pick up your toys instead of arguing, or it's responding with kindness when someone says something hurtful to you.

Proverbs 25:28 says if you don't have self-control, you are *"like a city with broken-down walls."* A city surrounded with walls is protected from an enemy's attack. If an enemy was able to knock the walls down, the city would be left unprotected. If the city's walls were never rebuilt, the enemy could always get in. So, if you don't have self-control, this means you don't have any protection against temptation. It means you could give in to all types of sin, like anger, disobedience, meanness, selfishness, and unkindness! This is why self-control is so important! When you live according to the Spirit, God will help you have self-control.

Think About It

How can you practice self-control in your life?

My Decrees

- I decree that I will not allow my emotions and feelings to control me.

- I decree that I will protect myself from this by keeping built up in prayer and the Word.

- I declare that I will allow Holy Spirit to help me live in such a way that pleases You and brings You glory.

- Thank You for teaching me self-control.

13 PROTECTION

"This I declare that about the Lord: He alone is my refuge, my place of safety; he is my God, and I trust him."
(Psalm 91:2 NLT)

When you chose to follow Jesus, many promises were given to you. Protection was one of those promises. Psalm 91 says that God is your refuge. A refuge is simply a safe place.

Have you ever been inside nice and cozy while a storm was going on outside? It is nice to be protected from the wind and rain! Sometimes scary situations in your life can be called storms. When you are scared, your first reaction might be to run. The place you should run to is God! He will keep you safe in scary situations and even protect you from sin when you trust Him. The Lord also says that His angels will help guard you. What a promise!

God wants to protect you and keep you safe because you are His child and He loves you. He wants to be a part of your life and is ready to answer anytime you are in need. Isn't it amazing to know God is protecting you? If you trust in God and call on Him to help you, He will!

My Decrees

- I decree that angels assigned to me the day I was born are surrounding me and protecting me.

- I declare that You watch over Your Word to perform it.

- I decree that I will trust that You are guarding me and keeping me safe.

- I decree that You are my safe place.

- Thank You for Your protection.

14 HEALING

"For I am the Lord who heals you."
(Exodus 15:26 NLT)

God is known by many names in the Bible and one of those is "The God who heals." Most often when you think of healing, you think of a physical healing from a sickness or disease. While God does heal people from diseases, He also heals people mentally, spiritually, and emotionally.

The Bible has more than thirty stories of the sick being healed. In Bible times and today, some people are healed instantly and some are healed over time. When someone is made well instantly, that is called a miracle. For example, if a person who is blind is prayed for and can instantly see, that's a miracle! Other people may slowly get better over time. Both of these are awesome ways that Jesus heals! Whether you are praying for yourself or for someone else, trust and believe in the God who heals!

Think About It
How can you believe God for healing?

My Decrees

- I decree that God wants me to be healed.

- I declare that Jesus not only died for my sins but for my healing, and I receive it!

- I decree that You heal sickness and disease.

- I decree that You are more than enough for every need I have.

- Thank You, Jesus, for being my healer.

15 HOPE

"May the God of hope fill you with all joy and peace in believing, so that by the power of the Holy Spirit you may abound in hope."
(Romans 15:13 ESV)

Biblical hope means to confidently expect something good. Hope in Scripture is not like the world's definition. The world says, "I hope this will happen, but it probably won't." For example, you might think, *I hope I make the team, but I probably will not.* Biblical hope is much different. Biblical hope is looking forward to something with absolute confidence, expecting it to happen.

The awesome thing about God being your hope is that you know He is faithful and that He will keep all His promises. Romans 5:5 (ICB) says, *"This hope will never disappoint us."* When you're tempted to be sad about something going on in your life, you can pray and look to God. He will fill you with the kind of hope that can only come from Him.

Hope is what happens in your heart when you believe the promises of God. Believe He has good things for you and place your hope in Him!

Think About It

Why can you place your hope in God?

My Decrees

- I decree that my hope is in You, for You are faithful and hope never lets me down.

- I decree that my hope is in You and I can expect good things to happen.

- I declare that all things are possible with You on my side and I am overflowing in hope!

- Thank You for a good future filled with hope.

16 GOD WORKS ALL FOR YOUR GOOD

"And we know that all things work together for good to them that love God, to them who are the called according to his purpose."
(Romans 8:28 KJV)

This verse is an awesome promise from God. He will work all things for your good when you love Him and follow His ways. Sometimes you might go through a hard situation and wonder how God could make anything good from it, but if you love God you can trust that He can and will!

Think about the making of a cake. Most of the ingredients that go into a cake are not something you would want to eat on their own, like raw eggs, flour, or oil. But when those ingredients are mixed together they become something wonderful and delicious. God does the same thing with your life. Even things that on their own can seem bad, God knows how to put them together to make something good. If you love and put your trust in God, He will take all the yucky, difficult times and work it for your good and purpose!

Think About It

Why does God work things for your good?

My Decrees

- I decree that You are the God of turnaround, and even when it doesn't look like it, You are working!

- I declare that goodness and mercy operate in my life and anything the enemy tries to use against me will be turned around and used for Your glory.

- I decree that You are changing the bad things to good things.

- Thank You for working all things for my good.

17

GOD WILL NEVER LEAVE YOU

"Be strong and brave. Don't be afraid of them.
Don't be frightened. The Lord your God will go
with you. He will not leave you or forget you."
(Deuteronomy 31:6 ICB)

God will never leave you or forget about you. Isn't that amazing to think about? The God who created the whole world wants to be with you! Because you can't physically see Jesus, you might sometimes forget that He is with you. This verse promises He is always there for you! If you wake up from having a bad dream, Jesus is there. If your family goes through a hard time, Jesus will be there for you. If you did something wrong and are feeling worried, Jesus will not leave you.

It is important to remember how much God loves and cares about you. His presence with you means that you don't have to carry any troubles or worried thoughts on your own. The opening verse encourages you to be strong and brave, knowing that your God is with you. Trust in this awesome promise that you are never alone.

My Decrees

- I decree that You are with me every place I go.

- I decree that angels are present to turn ugly situations into lovely ones.

- I declare that You are with me. Even in my dreams, You never leave me.

- Thank You for always being with me.

18

SPIRITUAL ARMOR

"Put on all of God's armor so that you will be able to stand firm against all strategies of the devil."
(Ephesians 6:11 NLT)

The armor of God helps protect you against the devil's schemes and plans. It is not armor you can physically put on, but it helps you spiritually. Throughout Ephesians 6 you can read about putting on different pieces of the armor. Let's look at these different pieces and see what they represent.

Ephesians 6:14 (NLT) says to put on the *"belt of truth."* This means you should speak what is true and not be dishonest. Verse 14 (NKJV) also tells you to put on the *"breastplate of righteousness,"* which means doing what is right. *"For shoes, put on the peace . . . from the Good News,"* which means you will always be ready to share with people about the good news of Jesus (Ephesians 6:15 NLT). Having the *"shield of faith"* means you know what you believe and why you believe it (Ephesians 6:16 NLT). Wearing salvation as a helmet means Jesus has saved you from your sins (see Ephesians 6:17 NLT). *"The sword of the Spirit"* means you know what the Bible says and how to use God's Word effectively (Ephesians 6:17 NLT).

With the full armor of God on, you will be able to stand and fight in spiritual battles.

My Decrees

- I decree that every day when I get dressed, I will not forget to put on my spiritual armor as well.

- I declare that Your armor equips me to handle whatever comes my way and it will protect me.

- I decree that I am strong in You and I am ready for battle!

- Thank You for providing spiritual armor.

19

ANGELS

"Beware that you don't look down on any of these little ones. For I tell you that in heaven their angels are always in the presence of my heavenly Father."
(Matthew 18:10 NLT)

Angels are some of the greatest helpers God has given you. Have you ever heard of a guardian angel? Angels in the verse above is plural, which means you have at least two guardian angels assigned to your life. Isn't that amazing?

Before you were ever born, God wrote down a plan for your life. He made great plans for your future and destiny. There are no bad things planned for you by God. The enemy may try to plot against you, but God's planned future for you is filled with hope.

The angels assigned to your life were most certainly told about your destiny. The angels who are in Heaven in the presence of Jesus are also taught by Him what your purpose is. You have an amazing destiny written by God Himself, and angels have been assigned to help you fulfill it!

My Decrees

- I decree that angels are assigned to my life and will protect me wherever I go, defending me from all harm.

- I declare that angels help me to walk out the plans and purpose You have for me.

- I declare that angels are assisting my destiny to come to pass.

- I decree that angels are watching over me.

- Thank You for my angel helpers.

20

GRACE

"God saved you by his grace when you believed. And you can't take credit for this; it is a gift from God."
(Ephesians 2:8 NLT)

Grace is getting something great that you don't deserve. It is an incredible gift and promise from God.

One of the wonderful stories Jesus told was of the prodigal son in Luke 15. The story is about a son who decided to leave his father. He made his father give him his inheritance, and then he wasted all of it. The son ended up poor and hungry and went back to his father, very ashamed. His father had actually been looking every day for him to return! So when he saw his son walking back home, he ran out to greet him. The father loved his son so much, he showed grace and welcomed him back home without asking any questions.

Jesus said this is exactly how God feels about you. If you mess up in any way, you can ask for forgiveness, and God will give grace to you. You can also give grace to others by forgiving them. Being a graceful person is an awesome way to be like Jesus.

Think About It

What does the gift of grace mean?

My Decrees

- I decree that I walk in grace. It is your gift to me.

- I decree that You never give up on me.

- I decree that You give me exactly what I need when I need it.

- I decree that I receive Your mercy and I will extend your grace and mercy to others.

- Thank You for Your amazing grace.

21 HEARING GOD'S VOICE

"My sheep listen to my voice; I know them, and they follow me."
(John 10:27 NLT)

Listening for God's voice can be confusing. You don't really hear God's voice loudly speaking to you, so how do you hear it? Hearing God doesn't come from your ears. It comes from your heart.

One of the best ways to hear God is from the Bible. The Bible is God's Word and He speaks to you through it. To recognize God's voice you must spend time in His Word. Sometimes, God speaks to you through thoughts and ideas He puts in your head. For example, if someone's name pops into your mind, it might be God's way of telling you to pray for that person. If a Bible verse comes to your mind, God might be encouraging you with it or telling you to do what the verse says.

It is important to know the voice of God you're trying to hear will never go against what the Bible says. If you have a thought in your head that goes against the Bible, then that's not God. Take time to listen for God's voice; He promises you will hear from Him.

Think About It
In what ways can you hear God's voice?

My Decrees

- I decree that I am Your friend and I know Your voice.

- I decree that I will listen carefully for it and search out Your Word to speak to me.

- I declare that when You speak, everything changes.

- I decree that I will spend time with You to hear You more clearly. I will not follow the voice of a stranger.

- Thank You that I know Your voice.

22 RAINBOW PROMISE

"I have placed my rainbow in the clouds. It is the sign of my covenant with you and with all the earth."
(Genesis 9:13 NLT)

One of my favorite things to do after a rainstorm is to go outside and look for a rainbow. There's something so beautiful and inspiring about them. Did you know the rainbow is a symbol of a promise from God?

There was a man in the Bible named Noah and he had found great favor in God's eyes. The entire population of the world had become evil and wicked, and God decided to bring a flood to the earth to destroy everyone except Noah and his family. God told Noah to build a large boat called an ark. The ark needed to be big enough to hold one male and one female from every kind of animal and creature. It rained for forty days and nights, and water flooded the land. When the rain finally stopped and the land was dry enough, Noah and his family left the ark and let all the animals out to find a new home. Noah thanked and praised God for taking care of them.

God made Noah a promise He would never flood the earth again. God put a bright rainbow in the sky as a reminder of His promise. When you see a rainbow you can be reminded that God is faithful to His Word.

Think About It
What is God's rainbow promise?

My Decrees

- I decree that every rainbow is a sign to me of Your promise to always take care of me.

- I declare that I am in covenant with You and You are faithful.

- I decree that I will see Your goodness right here, right now.

- I declare that no one can keep Your promises from me.

- Thank You that You provide an ark of safety for me.

23 STRENGTH

"Each time he said, 'My grace is all you need. My power works best in weakness.' So now I am glad to boast about my weaknesses, so that the power of Christ can work through me. That's why I take pleasure in my weaknesses, and in the insults, hardships, persecutions, and troubles that I suffer for Christ. For when I am weak, then I am strong."
(2 Corinthians 12:9-10 NLT)

Have you ever shared about something you're proud of? In these verses Paul didn't boast about something great he did; he boasted about his weaknesses! Paul asked God to take away his problems several times but God answered him in a way he didn't expect. God said His grace was all he needed. That was all Paul needed to hear and he responded by actually calling his problem a gift.

Do you think your struggles can sometimes be a good thing? Paul's prayer didn't change his problem but it did change his attitude. God can, and will, sometimes remove your problems when you pray, but other times, He promises His grace will help you go through them. God's promise to Paul is also a promise for you. When you are weak, He is strong. Find your strength in Him!

Think About It

**How can God make you
strong when you're feeling weak?**

My Decrees

- I decree that my weaknesses make room for You to be made strong in me.

- I decree that it is Your power causing me to triumph in all things.

- I declare that when problems try to overwhelm me, Your strength rises up and brings in the win!

- Thank You that when I am weak, You are strong.

24 OVERCOMER

"I have told you all this so that you may have peace in me. Here on earth you will have many trials and sorrows. But take heart, because I have overcome the world."
(John 16:33 NLT)

Think about Jesus's last moments on the earth. In John 16 Jesus was with His disciples shortly before He knew He was going to die. He knew His disciples were going to be upset, so He spent some time talking to them about the future, telling them where and why He was going and made sure they knew they wouldn't be alone. Then He said in verse 33, "*Take heart. I have overcome the world.*"

Take heart means to be confident in a hard situation. "Be brave! You've got this!" There's also more to it. You don't have to be brave alone. You aren't fighting troubles alone. You can be courageous because Jesus showed you how to be. He died on that Cross and rose again three days later, proving that He can overcome anything!

Overcome means to win over something. God can, and will, overcome troubles in your life. That doesn't mean that you won't have any more troubles but it does mean that God will help you get through them.

Think About It

How does God help you overcome troubles?

My Decrees

- I decree that I am an overcomer by Your Word.

- I decree that I do not fear because there are more angels with me than those against me.

- I declare that there are no limits with You and You are more than able to give me courage, a strong heart, and the ability to overcome any trouble.

- Thank You that because of You, I am a winner!

ABUNDANT LIFE

"The thief comes only to steal and kill and destroy. I came that they may have life and have it abundantly."
(John 10:10 ESV)

Jesus came so that people could have a life in Him that is filled with purpose and joy. Abundant means more than you expect. You receive this abundant life the moment you accept Jesus as your Savior.

God wants you to have a satisfying, wonderful life. The opening verse also says that trouble doesn't come from God. Things that steal and destroy are from the devil. Jesus doesn't send those kinds of things to you.

If you're in the middle of a hard situation, be encouraged that God will be close to you. He is able to do and give so much more than you could ever think, if you believe in Him and follow His ways. An abundant life is not about having the things of the world. It's about having more than you need of peace, love, joy, goodness, and the rest of the fruit of the Spirit. Living abundantly means living for God and having His promises greatly fulfilled in your life.

My Decrees

- I decree that You are God Almighty and You always do more than I could ever ask or think.

- I declare that I live in the fullness of who You are. There are no limits in You.

- I decree that I live and move and have my being in You!

- Thank You that I live in Your abundance.

REDEMPTION

"In him we have redemption through his blood, the forgiveness of sins, in accordance with the riches of God's grace."
(Ephesians 1:7 NIV)

Redemption is when God takes something bad and makes it good. God loves to redeem painful, sad, broken times and make them better. Redemption can also be thought of as an exchange or paying a price for something. Before you were saved, you were a sinner. Jesus took your sin and shame upon Himself when He died on the Cross. He did that so you wouldn't have to!

When you asked Jesus into your life, He took away your sins and gave you a clean heart. He redeemed your dirty heart into a pure one. There will still be times you make mistakes and sin. Sin separates you from God. But Jesus stops the separation when you ask for forgiveness.

Through Jesus, brokenness can be repaired. Hopelessness can turn to hope. Fear can become bravery. Sad times can become joyful ones. Jesus is your Redeemer. He will fix broken situations in your life and make them whole. He will redeem you.

Think About It
What does it mean to be redeemed?

My Decrees

- I decree that Jesus, my Redeemer, makes everything new!

- I declare that He is Lord of my life and has created a clean heart in me.

- I decree that He has changed everything and made me whole.

- Thank You for redemption through Your blood.

27 FORGIVENESS

"But if we confess our sins to him, he is faithful and just to forgive us our sins and to cleanse us from all wickedness."
(1 John 1:9 NLT)

Have you ever done something wrong and needed to ask for forgiveness? It is a relief when someone offers you forgiveness. It means no bad feelings are being held against you. Forgiveness of sin is only possible through the blood of Jesus.

Sin is anything you do that goes against God's commands. When you mess up, don't try to lie about it. Jesus became very upset at a group of people in the New Testament because they tried to pretend they didn't have any sin. The truth is, everyone makes mistakes and sins at times. There's nothing you can do to hide from it or cover it up. Go to Jesus with your sin and ask for forgiveness. It doesn't matter how big your sin is or how bad you think it is, He will forgive you every time!

Just as Jesus forgives you over and over, He wants you to forgive others too. Be like Jesus, forgiving and kind. God loves you and is waiting for you with open arms.

Think About It
Why should you ask God for forgiveness?

My Decrees

- I decree that my heart is changed when I ask You to forgive me for anything I've done wrong.

- I declare that when I repent You are faithful to forgive and I can walk in right relationship with You.

- I declare that because You forgive I also have the ability to forgive others.

- Thank You for Your faithfulness to forgive me of my sins.

28

SALVATION

"For God so loved the world that He gave His only begotten Son, that whoever believes in Him should not perish but have everlasting life."
(John 3:16 NKJV)

The promise of salvation is a beautiful gift from God. God created the world and everyone in it, including you. He is the One in charge of how things work. He wants to have a relationship with you and others.

In the beginning, Adam and Eve sinned and that gave people the desire to choose wrong things. Everyone is a sinner and sin can't enter Heaven. However, God made a way for you to get to Heaven when His Son, Jesus, died for you. Because Jesus took your place, you now have a way to have a relationship with God and a way to Heaven.

The way of salvation is only through Jesus and it is actually very simple to do! The first thing you do is talk to God and admit that you are a sinner. Ask Him to forgive you. Tell Him that you believe Jesus died for you. Then confess that Jesus is Lord and that He is *your* Lord. Keep your trust in Jesus and do your best to live like Him!

Think About It

What does salvation mean?

My Decrees

- I decree that "Jesus loves me, this I know"! In Him, I have found the Way, the Truth, and the Life.

- I declare that I will live for You and follow You all the days of my life.

- I decree that I am part of the family of God!

- Thank You for saving me and changing my life.

SPIRITUAL INHERITANCE

*"Now you are no longer a slave but
God's own child. And since you are his
child, God has made you his heir."*
(Galatians 4:7 NLT)

Once you are saved you become a child of God. This means that you have an inheritance in Christ, and you can also be called one of His heirs. An heir is someone who has the right to receive everything that God has. What an amazing promise! Every blessing and benefit in the Bible belong to you.

If you've accepted Jesus as your Savior and Lord then you have become part of God's family. The Bible describes God as King and Lord. Jesus is also called King of kings and Lord of lords. You're a King's kid! This means all the promises God made in the Bible belong to you.

Part of being a King's kid is to share God's love and goodness with others. It also includes being bold in your faith and defending God's Kingdom. After all, it's your Kingdom too, as you have an inheritance in it! Remember, you are God's child and your value is priceless.

Think About It
What does being a child of God mean?

My Decrees

- I decree that as an heir of God, Your blessings chase me down and overtake me.

- I declare that I am a rightful owner of all Your promises.

- I declare that I am a King's kid and walk with confidence because of who You are.

- Thank You for making me one of Your heirs.

HEAVEN

"There is more than enough room in my Father's home. If this were not so, would I have told you that I am going to prepare a place for you?"
(John 14:2 NLT)

If you believe in Jesus then Heaven is an incredible promise of God. The Bible describes many wonderful things about it. In Heaven there will be no pain and no tears. Can you imagine that? The Scripture also says that it never gets dark in Heaven. God's glory is so bright that it stays light all the time.

The Bible is also very clear that if you've accepted Jesus as Lord of your life, then you will spend forever with Him in Heaven. Jesus said He was going to prepare a room for you in His Father's house, which is Heaven. That can be really hard to wrap your mind around! The most wonderful thing about Heaven is that Jesus will be there. All of your family and friends who believe in Jesus will be there too. Continue to trust, believe, and live for God, knowing that the promise of Heaven is yours.

My Decrees

- I decree that Heaven is real and the best is yet to come!

- I decree that because You are my Father, I will live forever.

- I declare that I may not quite understand it all but I know I'll be there!

- I declare that my home in Heaven is secured for eternity.

- Thank You for the promise of Heaven.

31 Decrees for America

"First, I tell you to pray for all people. Ask God for the things people need, and be thankful to him. You should pray for kings and for all who have authority. Pray for the leaders so that we can have quiet and peaceful lives— lives full of worship and respect for God."
(1 Timothy 2:1-2 ICB)

It is important to pray for your nation's leaders because they have to make decisions every day. Their decisions should reflect God's morals and values. As a follower of Jesus, your prayer is powerful and effective.

You can pray these decrees over America with the authority you have in Jesus. (If you live in another country, just say the name of your country in place of *America*.)

My Decrees

- I decree that America is God's nation!

- I decree that we have no king but Jesus!

- I decree that America will reconnect to original promises between God and our founding fathers. Secret government plans will be exposed!

- I decree that God will promote leaders who have His heart and remove those who do not!

- I decree that the church of King Jesus is rising in America to promote God's ways in all 50 states!

- I decree that the promotion of laws against God will be defeated. Laws based on God's values will win!

- I decree that the greatest revival in America's history will soon begin. Millions will come to Jesus!

- I declare that a cleansing of dirty values will come and good and honest behavior will be restored!

- I declare that liberty and freedom provided by our Creator will not be taken from us!

- I declare that America shall be saved!

OVERCOME
PROBLEMS

(Ages 7th Grade–12th Grade)

1 DEPRESSION

"You changed my sorrow into dancing."
(Psalm 30:11 NCV)

You were created with many emotions and some days you are going to feel sad. You may even describe it as feeling down about things. Depression negatively affects how you feel, think, and act. The Bible may not use the actual word *depression,* but it does use words such as *downcast, broken-hearted, troubled, miserable, despairing,* and *mourning.*

The Bible also tells us about amazing men and women who really struggled. Even Jesus expressed His feelings of betrayal, sadness, and disappointment, and He is God! God is not going to judge you if you're feeling down. David wrote many psalms that go back and forth between him feeling down and then reminding himself that God was with him and for him. Everything changed for David when he started talking to God and God can do the same for you.

When you are feeling overwhelmed, talk to God about it, read your Bible, and worship Him. As you do, you will begin to feel His presence filling you with joy.

Think About It

**How can God help you with your feelings?
What are some things you can do when
you're feeling overwhelmed?**

My Decrees

- I decree that I will not live in depression. It will not overtake me.

- I declare that when I begin to feel troubled I will run to You because that is where my help comes from.

- I will encourage myself by praying in the Spirit and declare You have given me everything I need to overcome all things.

- I decree that I am complete in You and no good thing do You withhold from me, and that includes Your strength, peace, and joy.

- Thank You that Your mercies are new every morning.

2

FEAR

"Don't be afraid, for I am with you."
(Isaiah 41:10 NLT)

When you were younger you may have been afraid of the dark or thunderstorms or being alone. If any of those fears happened, you probably went to your parents' room or maybe to a sibling's. Fear is a very real and powerful emotion. As you have gotten a little older, you may have different fears: fear of the unknown, your future, or what others think of you. The list could be quite long. The Bible has much to say about fear and being afraid.

First John 4:18 says you can be tormented by your fear, but God's love takes the torment away. When you became a Christian, you received the gift of the Holy Spirit, and the Holy Spirit is God. That means God is with you wherever you are. God knows you will have moments of being fearful. That is why the Scriptures say over and over again, *"Do not be afraid."*

God reminds you again and again that He is always with you. Think about the situations that make you afraid and picture yourself facing those situations with God. The reality is you do not face those situations alone and God is greater than your fears.

Think About It

What times are the hardest for you to remember not to be afraid? How does it make you feel knowing God is with you?

My Decrees

- I decree that I do not walk in fear. It has no hold on me.

- I decree that even if it looks like or feels like I am surrounded, I am surrounded with Your love and Your power.

- I shake off every lie and the torment of fear and declare that in You I have victory, and it is Your perfect love that drives away fear.

- You are always faithful and You watch over Your Word to perform it.

- Thank You for being more than enough. Thank You that Your angels are with me!

3 FAILURE

"This is what the Lord says: When a man falls down, doesn't he get up again? And when a man goes the wrong way, doesn't he come back again?"
(Jeremiah 8:4 ICB)

Did you know the first chocolate chip cookies made were actually a mistake? Kenneth and Ruth Graves Wakefield owned and operated the Toll House Inn in Massachusetts. Ruth wanted to bake chocolate cookies for the guests but discovered she was out of baker's chocolate. To improvise, she chopped up a Nestle semi-sweet baking chocolate bar, thinking that the chocolate would melt and spread into the batter. The chocolate didn't melt into the batter, however, it just softened.

Although it wasn't what she was planning, Ruth served the cookies and they quickly became a hit. She eventually reached a deal with Nestle and the company began printing the "Toll House Cookie" recipe on their packages while supplying Ruth with all the chocolate she needed. What a sweet mistake! What started out as a failure turned into great success!

Sometimes the things you try to do in life don't turn out the way you thought they would. When that happens it is easy to want to give up. Don't give up! Give it to God. He can help turn any failure into success.

Think About It

What should I do if I feel like giving up?
How can I give my mistakes to God?

My Decrees

- I decree that there is a plan for my life and it will not fail! I will push through any disappointments or times I feel like giving up.

- I declare that even my mistakes can turn for my good.

- I declare that God and His angels are assisting my destiny and purpose even when things don't turn out the way I expected.

- Thank You that even mistakes can become sweet.

PEER PRESSURE

"Don't copy the behavior and customs of this world, but let God transform you into a new person by changing the way you think. Then you will learn to know God's will for you, which is good and pleasing and perfect."
(Romans 12:2 NLT)

You have probably experienced peer pressure in your life. While peer pressure can sometimes be positive, as in your friends encouraging you to study harder or practice more, it is usually negative.

Negative peer pressure is when your friends are encouraging you to do things that are wrong or make you feel really uncomfortable. You become worried that if you don't do what your friends want you'll be left out. Peer pressure is really hard! You want people to like you so it's hard to say no when they want you to do things, even if those things are wrong!

The Bible has some great insight into facing peer pressure. As a Christian, God wants you to honor Him by living a life that pleases Him. You're not meant to look like worldly people; you are meant to look like Jesus. Your foundation is God's Word. It shows you what is wrong and right so that you can be prepared to take a stand when pressure comes.

Think About It
How have you experienced peer pressure?
How can you make a stand for God?

My Decrees

- I decree that I will not be pressured into doing the wrong thing.

- I decree that I will make a strong stand for always doing what is right in Your eyes.

- I declare that I will not conform to what everyone around me is doing.

- I decree that my actions will line up with what God's Word says.

- Thank You for helping me change the way I think and teaching me how to walk in Your will.

5 ANXIOUS

"Don't worry about anything; instead, pray about everything. Tell God what you need, and thank him for all he has done."
(Philippians 4:6 NLT)

Worry is when you allow your mind to dwell on actual or potential problems. The things you worry about are either going to happen or not; worrying doesn't change the outcome. The Bible tells us in Romans 5 that worry doesn't add any time to our lives. In fact, it does the opposite! Worrying causes you to miss out on life. You probably worry about friends, grades, opinions, or even your future plans. These things are important, but if you spend your time worrying about them you're acting as if Jesus won't take care of you.

It is clearly told in God's Word not to worry but to place your focus somewhere else. And that "somewhere else" is seeking God's Kingdom and His righteousness. After that, everything will fall into place exactly how it should. When you worry, you're not letting God take care of things. Jesus tells us we can trust Him and you know He always keeps His promises. Pray and give your worries to God.

Think About It
Why do you think God tells you not to worry?
What can you do when you're feeling worried?

My Decrees

- I decree that my trust is in You. I will not worry.

- I declare that You are my way maker. I will not worry.

- I declare that my confidence is in You to work on my behalf regarding everything that I face.

- Thank You for keeping Your promises. I know You've got this!

6 DIFFICULT CIRCUMSTANCES

"You meant to hurt me, but God turned your evil into good."
(Genesis 50:20 NCV)

There are many things that may weigh heavy on your heart. School pressures, relationship drama, insecurities, problems at home, or worries about your future can make life feel overwhelming sometimes. You don't have to figure things out on your own. God is always there for you and He wants to help you see His goodness, even in difficult circumstances.

God uses tough times in our lives to change us and make us more like Him. The Apostle Paul is an awesome example of this. He faced lots of tough times in his life. He was shipwrecked, beaten, left for dead, and put in prison. Despite all the hard things that happened in his life, he kept a good attitude. He chose to put his trust in God and kept a positive attitude in the midst of hard times.

No matter what is going on around you, be comforted in the fact that God never leaves you and isn't the source of tough times. You can go to God and let Him be your shelter and refuge. Choose to look to God for His strength in difficulty. Remember that with God on your side you can't be defeated. Keep a good attitude and know God will help you through any difficulty you're facing!

Think About It

How can I see the good in tough times? How can I allow God to help me when life is hard?

My Decrees

- I decree that I am an overcomer!

- I declare that nothing the enemy throws against me will prosper because that is what Your Word says.

- I decree that no matter what I go through, You are more than enough and You never leave or forsake me.

- Thank You for making me a winner!

7 ANGER

"Always be willing to listen and slow to speak. Do not become angry easily. Anger will not help you live a good life as God wants."
(James 1:19-20 ICB)

Everyone gets angry sometimes. You may have not received a good grade on your science test, you could be angry because you see someone at your school getting bullied, or perhaps you've gotten angry because someone got a position on the soccer team and you didn't. Anger in itself isn't necessarily bad, but if you allow your anger to consume you, you can do things you regret.

What do you do when someone gets something you feel is unfair? Do you talk about them behind their back? Or maybe try to get even with them? Doing these types of things might make you feel better in the moment, but they are not the right way to respond to anger. If you find yourself struggling with anger, ask God for His wisdom and help. He can show you a practical way to deal with your anger. Or He might show you that you need to forgive someone who has done you wrong. He may show you a verse to help give you perspective on your situation. He wants to provide you with the help you need to overcome. Don't be afraid to ask for God's help.

Think About It

When is anger a sin? What are some things you can do when you're angry?

My Decrees

- I decree that I will not allow anger to control me and cause me to do unwise things or have reactions that are not pleasing to You.

- I declare that I will look to You for Your help when feelings try to erupt and take over my life.

- I declare that I will walk daily in Your love and Your mercies and not be ruled by my flesh.

- Thank You for helping me to deal with any anger in my life.

8 FEEL STRESSED

*"Cast all your anxiety on him
because he cares for you."*
(1 Peter 5:7 NIV)

Under stress you may feel tense, nervous, or on edge. The stress response is physical too. When you're nervous or stressed you might also feel your heartbeat or breathing get faster, your palms get sweaty, or your knees get shaky. There are many reasons you may become stressed. Perhaps you have a big test coming up, your sports schedule doesn't leave you time for anything else, or you may be worried about a friend situation.

There are practical and spiritual ways to ease your stress. Some practical ways include making time to simply relax, schedule fun activities you enjoy, solve the problems you can, and look for ways to manage your time better. Most importantly, when everything is feeling out of control and you are overwhelmed, talk to God about it. You don't have to handle everything on your own. In fact, God wants you to give your concerns to Him because He cares so much for you! Remember, worrying doesn't accomplish anything, but praying does. God doesn't want you to feel troubled. When you pray, He will fill you with peace. Life is easier to manage when you keep your eyes on Him.

Think About It

What are the things that make you feel stressed?
Why does God care about your worries?

My Decrees

- I decree that I'm resting in Your peace in every situation of my life.

- I declare that Your mercies are new every morning and I will give the day to You.

- I declare that I lay everything at Your feet that feels overwhelming to me.

- Thank You for caring so much for me.

9 SELF-IMAGE

"But God told Samuel, 'Looks aren't everything. Don't be impressed with his looks and stature. . . . God judges persons differently than humans do. Men and women look at the face; God looks into the heart.'"
(1 Samuel 16:7 MSG)

O ur culture can be obsessed with body image. From a young age you have been bombarded with what the world says is beautiful. It can be easy to think you don't measure up. You may even have a list of things you wish you could change about yourself. This is why it is crucial to know what God thinks of you. There are many amazing words God would use to describe you—words like *loved, child of God, beautiful, strong*, and *unique*.

Psalm 139 says you are fearfully and wonderfully made. It is important to take care of the body God created for you. Living a healthy lifestyle through eating well, getting enough rest, and exercising are all vital in maintaining your physical body. However, God is far more concerned with your inside than your outer appearance. He wants you to keep your heart and mind focused on Him so that you become a true reflection of who He is. See yourself as God sees you: a beautiful, wonderful masterpiece.

My Decrees

- I decree that I will not allow negative thoughts about my looks to overtake me, and societal pressures to conform will not overwhelm me.

- I declare that I am made in Your image and I will not compare myself to others.

- I decree that I will maintain my outer appearance but my focus will be on the "real" me, my heart, and pleasing You in the things I do and say.

- I thank You that You are the source of my confidence.

10 ENVY

*"Let us not become conceited, provoking
or envying each other."*
(Galatians 5:26 NIV)

Have you ever wished your life was more like someone else's? Envy is when you feel unhappy because you want what someone else has. Being envious does not glorify God and it actually breaks one of His Ten Commandments, which says, *"You shall not covet"* (Exodus 20:17 NKJV). That means that you shouldn't want what someone else has. If God thought this was important enough to include in the Ten Commandments, then it should be important to you too!

If you find yourself longing for someone else's life or what they have, the first thing you can do is pray and ask God to help change your feelings. Another way to combat envious thoughts is to purposely look for all the things you are grateful for in your life.

While it is not wrong to have goals or to desire good things in your life, it is wrong to specifically want what already belongs to another. Instead of desiring what someone else has, recognize that God has gifted everyone uniquely and be excited about His plan for you.

Think About It

Why do you think God doesn't want you to be envious? What can you do if you are feeling envious?

My Decrees

- I decree that I have a thankful heart and I do not allow jealousy or envy to enter it.

- I declare that I will be content in what You have done and are doing in me.

- I declare that You are helping me to be the best version of me.

- I decree that I am trusting God to give me my own blessings.

- Thank You for Your plans to bless me.

11 REJECTION

"I prayed to the Lord, and he answered me. He freed me from all my fears."
(Psalm 34:4 NLT)

Rejection hurts. It could be something small, such as no one saving you a seat at the lunch table or the person you like passing you without saying hello. Or it could be a bigger situation like not making the team you desired or not getting into the college of your choice.

Rejection can make you feel unwanted, unworthy, and undeserving. It can cause fear and doubt to overtake your emotions. It is important to remember that your value and worth are based in God. Your source of acceptance comes from Him. The enemy wants to twist any rejection you face by causing you to become fearful that God doesn't have good planned for you. Psalm 34:4 says, when you pray to God, He will free you from those fears and that irrational thinking. The truth is you are loved, chosen and desired. Focus on God and His promises for you.

Think About It

When have you have felt rejected? How can God help you overcome your feelings?

My Decrees

- I decree that no spirit of rejection can take hold of my life.

- I decree that I am completely accepted and chosen by You and You have promised You have plans and a future for me.

- I declare that even when disappointed in an outcome, I will continue to trust You are ordering my steps.

- I refuse fear and I declare that You are healing any hurts that have come against me because of rejection.

- I thank You that I am Yours and You are more than enough!

SELF-ESTEEM

"'And you must love the Lord your God with all your heart, all your soul, all your mind, and all your strength.' The second is equally important: 'Love your neighbor as yourself.' No other commandment is greater than these."
(Mark 12:30-31 NLT)

H ave you ever thought about whether you love yourself? Our opening Bible verses clearly state we are to love God with all our heart, but it also says to love our neighbor as ourselves.

Self-esteem can be tricky. You don't want to think too highly of yourself but you also shouldn't think too lowly. It is easy to base your worth on your skills and abilities. The world bases your worth on what you can do; Jesus bases your worth on who you are.

It is normal to want to be loved, accepted, and considered valuable by others. But when you place your worth in others' hands, it will fluctuate. No one chooses his family, race, background, or physical make up. God determines all of these things and He made you for this time and for a specific purpose. Realize you are worthy and valuable because God created you. His love for you is unconditional.

Think About It

What is the difference between worldly self-esteem and godly self-esteem? Why does God love you?

My Decrees

- I decree that I am made in Your image, perfectly designed by You.

- I declare that I am worthy and valuable because You live in me, You created me, and Your love is unconditional.

- I declare that even when I don't "feel" it, You are still with me and my faith is in You.

- I thank You that I don't have to earn Your love. I just walk in it.

13

CONFIDENCE IN GOD

"And I am certain that God, who began the good work within you, will continue his work until it is finally finished on the day when Christ Jesus returns."
(Philippians 1:6 NLT)

Sometimes you may doubt God, especially in tough times. You may be facing situations that seem overwhelming or confusing.

There is an awesome story in Mark 4 about a time when the disciples were doubting Jesus. Jesus told his disciples He wanted to go to the other side of a large sea. As they were crossing the sea, Jesus fell asleep in the boat. The wind and the waves began to get very strong as a storm began. The disciples were very afraid their boat was going to sink and they rushed to wake Jesus, asking Him why He didn't care that they were going to drown. Jesus got up and told the storm to be still and it obeyed! The disciples couldn't believe the wind and the waves listened to God's voice!

A storm can represent anything you face that is undesirable in your life such as problems, sickness, obstacles, or temptation. God has a solution for all the storms of life. You can be confident that He will see His plans for your life fulfilled. He will always be there for you.

Think About It

What are some storms that you have faced in life? How has God been there for you?

My Decrees

- I decree that my confidence is in You and You alone and You are where my strength comes from.

- I declare that no matter what I am going through or facing, You are with me and You never leave or forsake me.

- I declare that Your plan for me gives me a future and a hope and I will not back down.

- Thank You for having a solution for every storm.

14 DECISION MAKING

"Seek his will in all you do, and he will show you which path to take."
(Proverbs 3:6 NLT)

Have you ever struggled with making a decision? Or maybe you made the decision but it was the wrong one? It can be hard sometimes to know what to do, but God's Word gives some awesome ways to help guide you. Whether it's who to date, what class to take, or what team to try out for, God is interested in helping you make a decision. It begins by spending time with Him. You do this by reading the Bible and talking to Him. You will get to know God more and get His take on what choice you should make.

When you are trying to make the right decision, think about what Jesus values. You can make your decisions on what He thinks is important. Fix your thoughts on what is true, good, and pure and you will make your choice based on God's standards. You're actually training your mind to think about the right things so that when you are faced with a choice, you will know what to do. Set your mind on the things of God and you will make the right decision.

Think About It

What will help you make the right decision? How can God help you?

My Decrees

- I decree that You will speak to me and make my pathway clear.

- I decree that You will help me make wise decisions.

- I decree that I will trust You to guide my steps and lead me the right way.

- Thank You for always showing me what to do.

RESPONSIBILITY

"The master said, 'Well done, my good and faithful servant. You have been faithful in handling this small amount, so now I will give you many more responsibilities. Let's celebrate together!'"
(Matthew 25:23 NLT)

You probably have certain things you are responsible for such as chores around the house, making sure your homework is done, or doing your laundry. Responsibility is simply being in charge of something.

It is good to take care of things you've been given and recognize the blessings these things are in your life. Being responsible isn't just about how you care for your things, though; it is also about your behavior. You are responsible for your actions. You are also responsible for what you say and even what you think. This is a hard one! The things that you say and do start with your thoughts, and what you think comes from your heart. Take responsibility for those things. It's not always fun, but it will help you grow into a person of character.

You're the person responsible for where you are in life and your relationship with God. God has given you so much and one of the best ways you can thank Him is to be responsible.

My Decrees

- I decree that I will live my life responsibly.

- I decree that I will be careful in what I watch and listen to in order to guard my heart.

- I declare that I will read Your Word and let it renew my mind to build my character.

- Thank You for giving me so much and trusting me to be responsible.

16 Comparison

"Oh, don't worry; we wouldn't dare say that we are as wonderful as these other men who tell you how important they are! But they are only comparing themselves with each other, using themselves as the standard of measurement. How ignorant!"
(2 Corinthians 10:12 NLT)

When you compare yourself with others you either feel better or worse about yourself. Comparison can cause a feeling of insecurity or pride, and neither of those are good.

God put much thought and took great care in creating you. He has blessed you with unique looks, talents, skills and abilities. When you compare yourself to others and think you are lacking, you are disregarding the gifts God has given you. God placed you in your home, your family, and your church for a specific purpose. He never makes mistakes and He doesn't view anyone's looks, talents, or skills as more important or better than others.

You can free yourself from the act of comparison by remembering every good thing you have comes from God. Be thankful. Remember how special you are in the eyes of God. He loves you and has an incredible purpose for your life.

Think About It

How can Jesus help you not to compare yourself to others? What are some good things about you?

My Decrees

- I decree that I have been uniquely created and designed by God.

- I decree that I do not need to compare myself with anyone.

- I declare that it is You and You alone who has gifted me with specific traits.

- I decree that I will walk out my purpose and I will not be envious of others who are walking out their own paths.

- Thank You for what You are doing in my life!

17 DISCIPLINE

"No discipline is enjoyable while it is happening—it's painful! But afterward there will be a peaceful harvest of right living for those who are trained in this way."
(Hebrews 12:11 NLT)

Rules, rules, rules. You probably feel like you follow a bunch of rules at home, at school, at church, and everywhere you go. In this verse in Hebrews, discipline means training. In this context God is training His children. Much like your parents had to teach and train you to look for cars before crossing the street or to not touch a hot stove, God also trains you. Your parents taught you these things out of their love for you and God also lovingly disciplines. He wants to train you to become more and more like Jesus.

Think of God kind of like a coach who practices, teaches, and corrects His players so they can be in their best shape for a game. God wants you in top shape to run this race of life He has prepared for you. Discipline is not punishment. When God disciplines it is to draw you back to Him and His ways. Remember, He only wants what is best for you!

Think About It

How can you follow God's ways? How is God's discipline different from rules?

My Decrees

- I decree that because God loves me, I will learn to accept and apply His training for me to live my best life in Him.

- I declare that I will run my race well because He is involved in every aspect of teaching and correcting me to be a winner in every realm.

- I decree that I will not rebel against His discipline but use it to keep moving forward.

- Thank You for Your correction and always wanting what is best for me.

18 CHANGES

"So don't worry about these things, saying, 'What will we eat? What will we drink? What will we wear?' These things dominate the thoughts of unbelievers, but your heavenly Father already knows all your needs. Seek the Kingdom of God above all else, and live righteously, and he will give you everything you need."
(Matthew 6:31-33 NLT)

Change is inevitable throughout life. You've changed grades each year, experienced new teachers and new friends. You've gone from baby to toddler to teen. You've likely experienced a number of changes in your life, some easier than others. It can be easy to focus on the challenges of change, but change can also be a blessing!

Whenever you face a change you want to be assured that you're going to be okay. In Matthew 6:25, Jesus lets you know He understands basic worries. He starts with food, drink, and clothing. The verse goes on to say He already knows your needs. You don't have to worry because God knows. God doesn't promise a problem-free life, but He does promise He knows what you're going through.

Whenever everything feels like it's unknown and changing, you can depend on God. He is your constant and when you draw close to Him, He will be there for you.

Think About It

What are some ways your life can change? What are some blessings that can come from change?

My Decrees

- I decree that I trust God to lead me through changes in my life and I will not allow fear to take hold of me because of these changes.

- I declare that His angels assist me in every detail and I loose them to assist with change.

- I declare that God's got me and I don't have to worry or wonder "how." He sticks closer to me than a brother.

- Thank You that any change You make is good.

INITIATIVE

"Suppose you see a brother or sister who has no food or clothing, and you say, 'Good-bye and have a good day; stay warm and eat well'— but then you don't give that person any food or clothing. What good does that do?"
(James 2:15-16 NLT)

Initiative is improving a situation without being asked to do so. It is seeing a problem and deciding how you can be part of the solution. Think about if you had a thousand dollars in the bank and just left it there. Would it do you any good? Not if you didn't take it out and use it on something you needed.

That's kind of like faith without action. Just wishing someone well doesn't do any good. Be the kind of person who sees a problem and then takes action. There are many problems in the world that can seem overwhelming, but the point is to try and figure out what you can do, not think about what you can't do. Of course, you know you can pray, but God also calls you to do something. You could even be the answer to your own prayer!

Be the friend to the one who needs a friend, volunteer your time at your local food pantry. Put action to your prayer! God loves to use His people to make the world a better place. Take the initiative and make good things happen!

Think About It
What are some things you could do for others?
What are ways you can take initiative?

My Decrees

- I decree that I will not be a bystander. I will be an action taker!

- I decree that when I see a need I will fill it the best I can.

- I declare that I will pray and I will be available for You to use to answer needs and solve problems.

- Thank You for helping me be a doer.

WATCHING YOUR WORDS

"Words kill, words give life; they're either poison or fruit—you choose."
(Proverbs 18:21 MSG)

Your words are powerful. They can bring life, joy, encouragement, hope, and healing. They can also humiliate and destroy if you do not carefully control their use. There are approximately 150 verses in Proverbs that are devoted to the tongue, our speech, and our words. Obviously, this is important. The tongue can be a great blessing that accomplishes good or it can be a weapon of destruction.

The power in your tongue is ruled by your choice. If you are struggling with math and say things like. "I'm so stupid. I'll never understand this," then you probably won't. However, if you choose to say, "This is hard, but I'm going to keep trying. I know I can figure this out," you will have a much more positive outlook on it.

Luke 6:45 (NKJV) says, *"Out of the abundance of the heart [the] mouth speaks."* Fill your heart with the truth of God's Word so that you speak words of life.

Think About It

What does it mean that words kill or give life?
With what words can you fill your heart?

My Decrees

- I decree that I will watch my words! I will be positive and not negative.

- I decree that in every situation I will choose to speak words of life, and I will not speak destructive words.

- I declare that I will renew my mind daily with Your Word so that nothing comes out of me that is not of You.

- I will guard my heart so that my words create life and not death.

- Thank You that Your words are powerful and produce success.

21 BITTERNESS

"Get rid of all bitterness, rage, anger, harsh words, and slander, as well as all types of evil behavior."
(Ephesians 4:31 NLT)

Bitterness is a feeling of sadness or anger toward someone who has hurt you. You know it is an issue if your feelings toward the person remain the same or even grow stronger. The Bible describes hurts as seeds that are planted in you. If the seeds grow, they turn into bitterness.

Sometimes bitterness can be referred to as "holding a grudge." Holding bitterness in your heart can make you an angry and resentful person. You may think you are justified in remaining angry, but it's causing you more harm than good. The only way to remove bitterness from your heart is through forgiveness. It can be very difficult to forgive someone who has truly hurt you, but it will be beneficial to your soul.

The Bible says to forgive others just as Jesus has forgiven you. Pray and ask God to remove any unforgiveness from your heart and replace it with love. Don't allow bitterness to take root in your life! Pray and forgive!

Think About It

In what ways have you been hurt? How can you forgive those who have hurt you?

My Decrees

- I decree that I will not allow bitterness to take root in me.

- I decree that I will not allow anger, wrong words, or any other evil behavior to live in my heart.

- I declare that I choose forgiveness and love, and I have no room for any other thing.

- Thank You, Lord, for making me whole. I am complete in You.

22

MY BROKEN FAMILY

"The Lord your God goes with you; he
will never leave you nor forsake you."
(Deuteronomy 31:6 NIV)

A broken family is never an easy thing to deal with. If you are experiencing this, you will have many different emotions and thoughts. Family was God's idea from the beginning of creation. When it is functioning it is one of life's greatest gifts, but when it is crumbling, it is devastating.

What do you do when the family you've always known becomes broken? The most important thing you can do is stay close to God. Don't allow the anger, sadness, and confusion to pull you away from Him.

Use this tough time to draw closer to Him. God can heal the hurt and pain inside of you that no one else can. He is able to be a father to you if yours isn't. He can be a friend if you feel alone. He will be faithful if you feel like no one else is there for you. He already knows your thoughts, so He can handle whatever you need to say! Remember, God loves you and will never leave or forsake you.

Think About It

How can God help you and your family?
What can you do during a tough time?

My Decrees

- I decree that Your love for me will keep me from feeling overwhelmed and forsaken during tough times in my family.

- I declare that I will run to You, not away from You.

- I declare that I will talk to You and You will be my Father and Friend.

- Thank You that You are with me. You will never leave or forsake me.

23 HONESTY

"Don't lie to each other, for you have stripped off your old sinful nature and all its wicked deeds."
(**Colossians 3:9 NLT**)

There are many reasons a person might lie. To escape punishment, to hide something, or to think it will protect someone are a few reasons that come to mind. However, none of these excuses make lying right. The ninth commandment in Exodus 20:16 (NIV) says, *"You shall not give false testimony against your neighbor."* In other words, you should not lie. Lying is a sin that God hates and will lead to others not trusting anything you say.

God is extremely concerned with the truth. He knows that lying can destroy character, hurting the one who tells lies as well as others. Situations often arise at school, on the sports field, at church, or at home where there is a temptation to lie or twist the facts in your favor. But what happens if you do that? You will live in fear that your lie will be exposed. Honesty is always the best policy, even if it hurts. If you are careful about what you say and strive to tell the truth, you will be a person that others can rely on.

Think About It

Why is being honest important? Has telling a lie ever benefited you in the long run?

My Decrees

- I decree that the enemy is the father of lies and there is no place for that in my life!

- I declare boldly that I will be a person of truth and honesty.

- I declare that I will be a person who can be trusted and who represents You in all I say and do.

- Thank You that saying the truth makes me free.

IMPERFECTION

*"For all have sinned and fall
short of the glory of God."*
(Romans 3:23 NIV)

I'm going to let you in on something. Even though you are a Christian, you are going to mess up sometimes. You are going to sin and need to ask for forgiveness. And that's okay! God is not calling you to be perfect. He is calling you to be teachable and have a willing heart.

The fact is no one is perfect except Jesus. All throughout the Bible, imperfect men and women were used to do great things for God. A classic example is David. David declared his faith in God and killed Goliath. He was also chosen to be king of Israel. But he blew it over and over again. He was deceitful at times and even a murderer. Yet, he was called *"a man after God's own heart"* (1 Samuel 13:14 NLT). God didn't give up on David because he made mistakes. He still loved him and wanted what was best for him.

God loves you and wants what is best for you too. If you make a mistake, ask God to forgive you and keep going. Being a Christian is a lifelong journey and He will help you every step of the way.

What can you do if you make a mistake? What do you think it means to be after God's heart?

My Decrees

- I decree that You never give up on me and I won't give up on myself.

- I declare that because of Your Word, I know I can come to You and confess any wrongdoing and be forgiven.

- I declare that I will learn from any mistakes I make and I will continue to follow You in all I do and say.

- Thank You that You love me even though I'm not perfect.

25 ADDICTIONS

*"I can do all this through him
who gives me strength."*
(Philippians 4:13 NIV)

The word *addiction* is usually synonymous with drugs and alcohol. While those can certainly be addictions, there are many other addictive habits such as playing video games, screen time on phones or computers, or binging on shows. Any habit that you can't control is an addiction.

Sometimes you might try to deal with problems, stress, or busyness of life by trying to escape. Watching a show or scrolling through your phone isn't bad in itself, but if it hinders you from taking care of responsibilities, then it becomes a problem.

At your age you are developing patterns that will take you into adulthood. If you can prioritize how you spend your time now, you can set yourself up for success. Instead of trying to escape through addictive habits, turn to God through prayer and reading the Bible. Like any other area of life, God can give you the strength to overcome whatever may be overtaking you. If it doesn't glorify God, don't do it!

Think About It

How can God help you overcome addictive habits in your life? What can you do instead of engaging in addictive habits?

My Decrees

- I break off any addictions in my life that try to control my time, thoughts, and actions.

- I decree that the fruit of self-control will operate in my life.

- I decree that I will set my priorities to seek You first and everything else in my life will fall into place.

- Thank You, God, for helping me break off addictions.

TEMPTATION

"The temptations in your life are no different from what others experience. And God is faithful. He will not allow the temptation to be more than you can stand. When you are tempted, he will show you a way out so that you can endure."

(1 Corinthians 10:13 NLT)

Life can be challenging and the temptations you face will, at times, be intense. A temptation simply means wanting to do, or have, something that you know you shouldn't. Being tempted is not a sin, but if you act on it, it could become one.

Thoughts that may lead you to temptation include, *Just one lie won't matter, No one will know,* or *Everyone else is doing it.* The beginning of 1 Corinthians 10:13 says your temptations are no different from anyone else's. Everyone faces temptations. The Bible says even Jesus was tempted! The verse goes on to say God will help you fight temptation and provide a way out.

When you are tempted with something, consider if it lines up with God's purpose and plans for you. If you need help, ask Him. He wants to give you the strength to resist temptation!

My Decrees

- I decree that God will help me overcome temptation.

- I decree that God will always make a way out of every temptation for me.

- I decree that I will not give in to temptation, no matter what anyone else is doing.

- Thank You for never allowing temptation to be more than I can handle. You will always help me.

DOUBT

"Then Jesus told him, 'You believe because you have seen me. Blessed are those who believe without seeing me.'"
(John 20:29 NLT)

I n the book of John there is a story about a man named Thomas. Thomas had been a disciple of Jesus for three years when Jesus was crucified and then resurrected. After Jesus rose from the dead, He appeared to all His disciples except for Thomas, who wasn't with the other disciples. The disciples later told Thomas about Jesus being alive, but Thomas had a hard time believing something he could not see.

Thomas is often referred to as "Doubting Thomas." He doubted the resurrection was true because he didn't see it. He refused to believe unless he saw Jesus for himself. It can be hard to have faith and trust in something you can't see. Jesus finally appeared to Thomas and his doubt transformed to faith the minute he saw Jesus.

Jesus promised, when you seek Him with all your heart, you will find Him. Don't allow doubt to stop you from seeking and believing in God. He will be there to give you faith!

Think About It

Is it sometimes difficult to believe in God when you can't see Him? What can you do if you are doubting God?

My Decrees

- I decree that even when I can't see it, You are working!

- I declare that by faith You are good and faithful, moving and operating behind the scenes on my behalf.

- I declare that my faith is greater than my doubt.

- Thank You that Your presence removes doubt from my life.

Broken Heart

"The Lord is close to the brokenhearted; he rescues those whose spirits are crushed."
(Psalm 34:18 NLT)

God knows there will be difficult, heart-breaking moments in your life. You may experience the loss of a loved one, a divorce in your family, or a rough battle with sickness. There may also be times when you are devastated over current world events or tragic news.

Psalm 34 was written by David, who suffered at times from fear, depression, and worry. He wrote verse 18 after he had escaped from the enemy once again. To escape from being killed, he pretended to be a crazy man by dribbling saliva down his beard. Can you imagine his desperation?

Psalm 34:18 in The Message Bible says, *"If your heart is broken, you'll find God right there; if you're kicked in the gut, he'll help you catch your breath."* When you are at your lowest moment, God steps in to be near. If you are brokenhearted, He will help heal you and put you together again. If your soul feels crushed, He will lift you up. God is always available to help you. You are not alone. God sees you and He loves you.

My Decrees

- I decree that when my heart is broken, You come close to me.

- I decree that You are the Great Physician and you mend my broken heart.

- I declare that You fill every void and broken place in my heart.

- Thank You that when I am crushed, You rescue me and help me catch my breath.

29

NEEDING DIRECTION/ GUIDANCE

"Your word is a lamp to guide my feet and a light for my path."
(Psalm 119:105 NLT)

There will be many times you wish you just knew the right thing to do. You may be trying to decide where to go to school, what sport to play, or who you should date. Decisions have consequences and you want to make the right one.

Our opening verse from Psalm 119 says that God's Word is a lamp to guide your feet and light for your path. It may seem like a more fun idea to do what you want, but God's Word should lead and guide you. When you don't know what the right choice is, read His Word. It will "light up" the decision you should make and the path you should take.

As you spend time reading the Bible and growing your relationship with Jesus, you will find making the right decision becomes much clearer. The Bible has answers to any circumstance or situation you may face. When you don't know what to do, it will show you. When you're not sure of the future, it will encourage you. God's Word is the answer!

Think About It
**How is God's Word like a light? In
what ways does God guide you?**

My Decrees

- I decree that I will look to You to guide my path.

- I decree that when I am faced with decisions and choices, I will trust You to make the way clear to me.

- I declare that wisdom operates in my life because I spend time in Your Word.

- I declare that I will seek Your face until I know that I know that I know!

- Thank You for helping me know.

30 FEEL DISCONNECTED FROM GOD

"Come close to God, and God will come close to you."
(James 4:8 NLT)

Life can get busy. You are involved in many different activities from youth group to sports to after school clubs. One day you wake up and think, *When was the last time I prayed or spent any time with God?* Your desire is to be close to Him but you got distracted. There are many ways you can reconnect.

Just like a friend you haven't talked to in a while, but as soon as you call it's just like old times, that's how it is with God. If you are feeling disconnected you can take steps to be closer. Simply open your heart to Him by reading your Bible, by praying, by attending church, and spending time in worship. The closer you stay with God, the easier it will be to go through life. He will help you stay on the right path to fulfill your purpose and the plans He has for you as you grow closer in your relationship with Him.

Think About It
What can you do if you're feeling disconnected?
How does staying close to Jesus help you?

My Decrees

- I decree that I will live under the shadow of Your wing and that You will be my hiding place and my shelter.

- I declare that I will press in to be closer and more connected in my relationship with You.

- I decree that I close the door to anything the enemy tries to use to come between us.

- Thank You that as I come close to You, You come close to me.

STEP INTO PURPOSE

(Ages 7th Grade–12th Grade)

1 PURPOSE

"You can make many plans, but the
Lord's purpose will prevail."
(Proverbs 19:21 NLT)

Purpose declares why you exist. It is the heart of why you are here on this earth. Just as a pen is used for writing, a book is meant for reading, and a guitar is for making music, God created you with a specific purpose in His mind. You were uniquely made with very special talents and gifts that the world needs. Before there was even one day to your life, God had amazing plans for you.

Thinking about how God has gifted you is a great way to discover what God might like you to do with your life. The gifts you have are like road signs to where God is directing you. You might be a great singer, artist, scientist, or athlete and all of these can play a part in how you serve God. As you look to the future, you can be confident that God promises amazing blessings for you!

My Decrees

- I decree that angels sent to reveal and draw out my God-given purpose—my God-given potential—be loosed in Jesus's Name.

- I decree that I was born for these times.

- I decree that the gifts, talents, and abilities God put in me are being anointed to reach new levels.

- Angels assigned to me the day I was born have been briefed concerning my purpose, and they are partnering with me to accomplish God's will for my life.

- Thank You that You will accomplish Your purpose in my life.

2 IDENTITY

*"I will praise You, for I am fearfully
and wonderfully made."*
(Psalm 139:14 NKJV)

Who am I? It is a question that is eventually asked by every-one. Identity is a clearly defined definition of self. As a Christian your identity is understood by your relationship with Jesus. It is important to know what the Bible says about your identity in Christ and not to allow society, peers, achievements, or failures to define who you are.

Part of your identity is wrapped up in the story of your life. Things that happen to you help shape and form the essence of who you are. As one who believes in Jesus, trust that He is helping write your story. Place the pen in His hands and see the wonderful things He has planned for you.

The Scriptures clearly explain that you were created in the image of God. You were given your identity so that God could be seen in you. You are to reflect His character so the world can know who He is. Your identity in Christ helps define your values, priorities, passions, and purpose.

Think About It

What is the purpose of your identity? How does believing in God help shape who you are?

My Decrees

- I decree that God uniquely designed me with characteristics to shape my identity in Him in order for me to walk out my destiny which He has prepared.

- I decree that I will not be influenced by current culture as to who I am, but I will be defined by who God says I am, according to His Word.

- I decree that the passions and purpose that God placed in me were written before I was even born. They are part of His design for my life and who I am to be.

- I decree that angelic assistance will help bring to pass all God has ordained for my life.

- Thank You, God, for continuing to write my story.

3 DESTINY

*"Before I shaped you in the womb, I knew
all about you. Before you saw the light
of day, I had holy plans for you."*
(Jeremiah 1:5 MSG)

Destiny is God's unique special plan for your life. He has a predetermined purpose that He created for you before you were even born. He took time to think about you and the Bible says He wrote amazing ideas for you before there was even one day to your life!

Remember, God designed you with special skills, talents, abilities, and personality traits, but you have a choice about what you do with those gifts. You must make the right decisions and choices to fulfill your destiny. Make choices that bring honor and glory to God. Part of your destiny is to be a child of God. You were created in His image and designed to be like Him.

You are extremely important and valuable to God. As you pray, listen, and obey His Word, He will help lead and guide you. Your destiny is good and your future is bright!

Think About It
What do you think God's special plan for your life is? How can you use your gifts to glorify God?

My Decrees

- I decree that angels who connect me to people, places, circumstances, events, and my purpose be loosed in Jesus's Name.

- I declare that He who has begun a good work in me will complete it.

- I declare that angels are here now connecting me to destiny assignments and protecting my purpose. They are wrestling destiny out of me.

- Thank You, God, that my future is bright.

4 POTENTIAL

"God can do anything, you know—far more than you could ever imagine or guess or request in your wildest dreams! He does it not by pushing us around but by working within us, his Spirit deeply and gently within us."
(Ephesians 3:20-21 MSG)

Potential is having the capacity to become something in the future. It is hidden ability, talents, or gifts that are not yet developed. For example, a professional musician or athlete wasn't just born that way. They put in many hours of practice and effort to become excellent.

God wants you to maximize the potential He has given you by you taking steps daily. If you are not practicing and working on the skills and talents you have, then you are living below your potential. God packaged things in you for the good of this world and has given you all you need to fulfill His plan and purpose. Set a goal and begin working on becoming better at the gifts God has given you. God wants you to reach your potential and He will give you the guidance and strength to accomplish it.

Think About It
What is a goal you can set for yourself
to help you reach your potential?

My Decrees

- I declare that my destiny is Holy Spirit empowered.

- I decree that God is working in me to reveal and produce my full potential to fulfill His purpose and plan for my life.

- I decree that the gifts, talents, and abilities God put in me are being anointed to reach new levels.

- I decree that angels who assist Holy Spirit in leading God's plan for my life before I was ever born are loosed in Jesus's Name.

- I decree that I will not waste my potential. I will become who I am supposed to be.

- Thank You, Lord, for helping me reach my potential.

5 CHOSEN

"Even before he made the world, God loved us and chose us in Christ to be holy and without fault in his eyes. God decided in advance to adopt us into his own family by bringing us to himself through Jesus Christ. This is what he wanted to do, and it gave him great pleasure."
(Ephesians 1:4-5 NLT)

I wasn't a big fan of school gym class. In particular, I didn't like waiting to be chosen for a team. I wasn't the greatest athlete and was usually one of the last ones picked. The world is sometimes cruel in how it chooses people. Thankfully, God is nothing like that!

To be chosen by God means you are His first and best choice. God chose you before He even created the world. He considers you special and set apart. The opening verses also say that He has adopted you. Adoption is a meaningful and special life-changing decision. Being in a family should mean receiving unconditional love without working to earn it. Typically, parents give their children what their children need simply because they are part of the family. You are also God's child and He gives you what you need because He loves you. He calls you His own and has a special plan for you.

Think About It
What does it mean to be chosen by God?
What does it mean to be adopted by God?

My Decrees

- I decree that I am chosen by God to be His child.

- I decree that I am a part of His family and unconditional love surrounds me.

- I decree that I was born "for such a time as this" and am called by His Name.

- Thank You for being my Father.

6 FUTURE

"'For I know the plans I have for you,' says the Lord. 'They are plans for good and not for disaster, to give you a future and a hope.'"
(Jeremiah 29:11 NLT)

This verse was written to a group of people who were being held captive. They were being reminded that even though they weren't where they expected to be, God had not forgotten about them. Even in very hard situations, God's plans still stand. His plans are always good.

The future can sometimes seem scary because there are so many unknowns, but God holds your days in His very capable hands. You may not know how your destiny is going to unfold, but He does. You may be wondering how your purpose is going to be fulfilled, but God already has the plan in place. There will be times that things happen in your life that take you by surprise. God is never taken by surprise. His Word says that He knows the end from the beginning. You can trust Him with your life and be confident He is always there for you. Look forward to a hope-filled future!

My Decrees

- I decree that angels who go ahead to prepare my way for success be loosed in Jesus's Name.

- I decree that I am strong in the Lord and in the power of His might.

- I declare that God has placed a future and a hope before me and they're both good.

- I decree that because You know the future, I trust You.

- I thank You, Lord, that nothing takes You by surprise. My life is in Your hands.

7 FRIENDSHIPS

"The righteous choose their friends carefully." (Proverbs 12:26 NIV)

God wants us to show kindness to others, but it's also extremely important to choose your friends carefully. Good friends are vital to your life and the Bible talks about the importance of true friendship. A true friend shows love, gives great advice, brings joy to your life, doesn't gossip about you, is loyal, forgives without holding a grudge, and helps you in time of need.

Friendship can have its negative aspects as well. Supposed friends can lead you into sin or a friend can lead you astray spiritually. People you thought were friends can prove false, deserting you when your friendship no longer benefits them. Your friends' attitudes and personalities also rub off on you. Little by little, you become more and more like the people who surround you. That's why it's so important to surround yourself with positive influences.

Pray that God would bless you with good friends that will encourage, love, and support you. Also know the greatest friend you could ever have is Jesus and He is glad to call you His friend.

Think About It

Why is it so important to choose your friends carefully? What are some ways you can be a true friend?

My Decrees

- I decree that Holy Spirit boldness over my life to empower me to set a standard for godly friendship.

- I declare that wisdom operates in me when I am with my friends and when I am choosing friends.

- I declare that God will bring good friends into my life.

- I decree that that Holy Spirit will govern my life and my relationships.

- I thank You, God, for good friends.

8 WORSHIP

"You are worthy, O Lord our God, to receive glory and honor and power. For you created all things, and they exist because you created what you pleased."
(Revelation 4:11 NLT)

Very simply, worship is spending time with God. It's a way to focus on Him and who He is.

A magnifying glass is used in order to see something better. The glass does not change the actual image, but it makes the image clearer. The object you are looking at does not actually change in size. What changes is how you see it.

When you magnify God through worship and praise, you are not changing anything about who God is. What you are doing is taking a closer look at His attributes—who He said He is through His Word. True worship is a heartfelt expression of love, admiration, fascination, wonder, and celebration. It's something that happens in your heart and soul when you begin to praise God for who He is and thank Him for what He's done. He is deserving of your praise and worship and you will be amazed how your problems seem so small in His presence.

Think About It

**What are some ways you can magnify God?
Why does He deserve your worship?**

My Decrees

- I decree that I will worship Him in all I do and say.

- I declare that no matter how I feel, God is worthy to be praised and I will always praise Him.

- I declare that in good times and bad times, I will honor God and I will declare His awesomeness all the time!

- Thank You for who You are and Your presence in my life.

9 WITNESS

"But you will receive power when the Holy Spirit comes upon you. And you will be my witnesses, telling people about me everywhere—in Jerusalem, throughout Judea, in Samaria, and to the ends of the earth."

(Acts 1:8 NLT)

Sharing about Jesus with others can seem intimidating, but being a witness is an important part of your purpose. One of the best ways to share Jesus is by showing others His characteristics. You are made in His image and are a reflection of Him. Be friendly, kind, encouraging, and supportive. Stick up for someone who's being picked on and pray for anyone who needs healing.

Be a student of God's Word so you can effectively share about Him with others. Talk about church and invite friends to your youth group or special events. The best witness is one who lives what they are sharing, so be mindful of your words and actions. Use your life to help point others to Jesus.

Think About It

What are some other ways you can think of to be a witness for Jesus? Why is being a witness important?

My Decrees

- I decree that Holy Spirit boldness operates in my life and I will do my best to represent Jesus in all I say and do.

- I loose angels to lead me to unbelievers who are ready and receptive to Jesus.

- I declare that God is helping me every day to be strong in my faith, to be sensitive to those around me who may need help, and to live what I believe.

- Thank You for opportunities to share You with others.

10 COURAGE

"This is my command—be strong and courageous!
Do not be afraid or discouraged. For the Lord
your God is with you wherever you go."
(Joshua 1:9 NLT)

There are many things that can make you feel afraid. It could be fear of the future, worry about failing your history test, or fear that your crush will reject you. Everyone deals with fear at some point in their life. Even though fear is something we all face, if we let it, fear will stop us from doing the things God wants us to do.

The bad thing about fear is that if you give in to it, you'll find yourself unhappy and living with regrets. So instead, you must choose to be strong and courageous. Joshua 1:9 says, *"The Lord your God is with you wherever you go."* This means being strong and courageous are not based on your ability to be strong and courageous, but on God's. You can stand against fear when you know God is with you.

Remember, regardless of what you're facing, God has a plan for you. Don't allow fear to stop you from doing what God has called you to do.

Think About It

**In what area of life do you feel like
you need some strength or courage?
How can you have more courage?**

My Decrees

- I decree that fear is a liar and the Greater One abides in me.

- I decree that I will choose to be strong and courageous.

- I declare that I am an overcomer through the power of God.

- I decree that I am not afraid or discouraged for God is with me wherever I go.

- Thank You, God, for filling me with Your courage.

11 WISDOM

"For the Lord gives wisdom; from His mouth
come knowledge and understanding."
(Proverbs 2:6 NKJV)

Wisdom is an important part of living life God's way. You may think the word *wisdom* means being smart, but biblical wisdom is much different. It means knowing what is right and actually doing it.

The Bible should be your source for wisdom and God's Word describes two types. The person with wisdom that comes from Heaven is peace-loving, considerate, submissive, and merciful, producing good fruit. But the person with the other kind of wisdom—worldly wisdom—is selfish, ambitious, envious, and disordered, practicing every other evil.

Hearing, reading, studying, memorizing, and meditating on the Word of God will help you to live a good life and make the right choices. It may seem easier to make choices based on what you want to do, but it is always best to rely on God for the best thing to do in a situation. Even if what you want to do is different, trust that God's way is better. Respect and have faith in God that He knows what He is doing and that His plan is the right plan for you.

Think About It

Why is wisdom important?
How can you gain wisdom?

My Decrees

- I decree that I walk in the wisdom of God and His blessings as I learn to honor His Word.

- I declare that the fear of the Lord is the beginning of knowledge, but fools despise wisdom and instruction.

- I decree an open heart for God's wisdom so that I do not fall into any of the enemy's traps or pits.

- Thank You, God, for giving me wisdom and understanding.

12 FEAR OF THE LORD

"'For I am a great king,' says the Lord Almighty,
'and my name is to be feared among the nations.'"
(Malachi 1:14 NIV)

The "fear of the Lord" is a frequently used phrase in the Bible. The word *fear* has a different meaning in this phrase than what is typically thought. Usually, *fear* is a word used if you are feeling afraid. In this context, it means utmost respect, honor, or reverence.

To fear the Lord you must know who He is. The more you know who God is, the greater you will love Him and want to show Him respect. God is good. God is love. God is kind and He wants what is best for you and your life. But that doesn't mean you shouldn't take Him seriously. You should care about what He thinks. Often, it is easier to care more about what your friends think than what God thinks, but it is vitally important to consider Him and His ways. Some questions to ask are, "What does God think about this decision I'm about to make?" Or "What would Jesus do in this situation?" That's the path to true wisdom and understanding.

You don't have to be afraid of God, but you should definitely be concerned about what He thinks. Fear of the Lord means basing your actions on your love and respect for Him.

Think About It

What can you do to learn to fear the Lord?
Why would fearing God help you make wise choices?

My Decrees

- I decree that I will walk in the fear of the Lord.

- I decree that my lifestyle will line up with God's Word and I will bring Him honor.

- I declare that I will choose God's way in every area of my life.

- Thank You, God, for wanting what is best for me.

13 KNOWLEDGE

"The people who know their God shall be strong."
(Daniel 11:32 NKJV)

A. W. Tozer once said, "What comes into our minds when we think about God is the most important thing about us." You can have knowledge about many things from academics to sports to music. However, the knowledge you have about God is the most important.

The best way to know God more is to spend time with Him, read His Word, pray to Him, listen for His voice, and worship Him. As you get that history with God, He will reveal more of His character to you. As you grow, mature, and begin thinking about your future, there are important aspects of God to know.

Nothing you do can make God love you any less. He is always there for you and wants what is best for your life. He is always faithful. Knowing the truth of who God is will help you when uncertain times come. Knowing that He never changes will help ground and sustain you. You may not understand everything about life, but knowing God will fill you with strength.

Think About It
Who is God to you?
How can you know Him more?

My Decrees

- I decree that I will renew my mind with God's Word.

- I decree that the more I know Him, the greater the direction of my life will be.

- I decree that knowing the truth of who God is makes me strong.

- Thank You that I can know You.

OBEDIENCE

"He replied, 'Blessed rather are those who hear the word of God and obey it.'"
(Luke 11:28 NIV)

Many look at being a Christian as having to follow a bunch of rules or commands or a big list of things they can do and things they can't do. However, God's way of doing life is so much bigger and better than that.

Obedience means to hear God's Word and act accordingly. When you obey what God tells you to do, it should be done with a willing heart that understands that His direction for your life is given because He loves you. When you make certain decisions because you know it's what God would want you to do, you need to trust that He knows what's best. Sometimes that can be difficult. For example, someone tells a lie about you and instead of retaliating, you show them love because the Bible says for you to do so. Or your friends are pressuring you to take something little from a store that no one would know about, but you know God said, "Don't steal."

It may not always be easy, but God will help you obey what He says. As a follower of Jesus, it's less about what you want and more about whom you love. Simply put, you obey God because you love Him.

Think About It

Why is it sometimes difficult to do what God says? What are some ways you can obey God?

My Decrees

- I decree that I will make a quality decision each and every day to obey God.

- I decree that I will give Him first place in every part of my life and I will do what He tells me to do.

- I decree that when I might miss it, I will repent and begin again.

- Thank You that I am blessed when I obey.

15 PERSEVERANCE

*"And let us run with perseverance
the race marked out for us."*
(Hebrews 12:1 NIV)

Have you ever wanted to just give up? Maybe on a sport, an instrument, or schoolwork? Perseverance is not for the weak. It is persisting in doing something despite difficulty. It's hard to press on when things are tough, but it's incredibly important.

When perseverance is necessary, it's usually because there's some sort of suffering involved: pain in an athletic practice, messing up over and over trying to get the notes right on your instrument, or making mistake after mistake on your math assignment. The suffering causes the need for perseverance.

Persevering through hard times builds character and causes hope. For example, in the middle of long races, runners may hit a point where they feel physically and emotionally spent. From their perspective, the finish line is far away and quitting is a strong temptation that they must overcome. When Christians continue running, choosing obedience over emotions, they will eventually experience hope rising in them because of a renewal of God's strength. You can persevere through anything because Jesus believes in you. He's walking right beside you and cheering you on!

Think About It

Has there ever been a time in your life when you had to choose whether to persevere or quit? Why is perseverance important?

My Decrees

- I decree that I have made a quality decision not to allow the forever loser to defeat me.

- I decree that I will walk with God throughout my life and angels will assist me.

- I declare that I am committed to run the race and will cultivate a life of perseverance and I will not quit.

- I decree that no matter if it is difficult or easy, I will pursue God and strive to please Him.

- Thank You for walking beside me and cheering me on.

SERVING

"For even the Son of Man came not to be served but to serve others and to give his life as a ransom for many."
(Matthew 20:28 NLT)

In His life on earth Jesus showed the importance of helping others. He did not serve others for anything He would get out of it; He served out of love.

As a follower of Jesus you are called to imitate the example Jesus set. Anyone can serve others, even a non-Christian. So what sets you apart? What set Jesus apart was that He came not only to serve, but also to give His life, which He accomplished through His death and resurrection. It's the life of faith you have in Him that sets you apart from others who serve. It's not simply doing something nice for someone.

The purpose behind your serving is about sharing the love of Jesus with people. Since God served you through His Son, Jesus, you can serve others in order to point them to Him. You don't have to make grand gestures, as people appreciate many types of service. For example, you could take out the trash without being asked, hold the door open for someone, or help a friend with homework. The point is to continue becoming more like Jesus and Jesus loves to serve.

Think About It

In what ways can you serve others?
Why is serving others important?

My Decrees

- I decree that I will serve the Lord both in big ways and in small ways.

- I declare that I will listen to Him each day for direction and opportunities He provides for me to make a difference.

- I declare that I will show His lovingkindness to everyone I meet.

- I declare that in everything I do I will give Him the glory and the honor and the praise.

- Thank You, Jesus, for the privilege of serving You.

17 CONSISTENCY

"Whatever is good and perfect is a gift coming down to us from God our Father, who created all the lights in the heavens. He never changes or casts a shifting shadow."
(James 1:17 NLT)

Consistency is always behaving the same way or having the same attitude toward something or someone. Consistency is the key to success in many areas of life. Consistent studying produces good grades. Consistent exercise leads to a healthier body. Consistency is also important in your relationship with God. Our opening verse assures us that God never changes; He is always the same. Isn't that comforting?

The consistency of God is important because it means He is always someone you can rely on and trust. Because God is consistent and the goal is to be more like Him, it is important for you to be consistent too. Consistency in your faith means you are the same person at home, church, or school. It requires a determined, disciplined effort on your part. Some ways to do this include creating and keeping a special time for prayer and reading the Bible. It would also include being consistent with attitude and behavior.

Be encouraged in your faith and know Jesus is the same yesterday, today, and forever. You can always count on Him!

Think About It

In what ways could you be more consistent in your walk with God? Why is consistency important?

My Decrees

- I decree that I will take comfort in understanding that God never changes.

- I decree that I will work on the discipline necessary to allow God to correct any areas of my life that need it.

- I decree that I will live my life consistent with God's Word.

- I thank You that You never change.

THANKFULNESS

"Always be joyful. Never stop praying. Be thankful in all circumstances, for this is God's will for you who belong to Christ Jesus."
(1 Thessalonians 5:16-18 NLT)

We read a lot about the life of David in the Bible. David was a shepherd who eventually became the king of Israel. David encountered some awesome times, yet he also had some very difficult experiences. No matter what he was facing, we read of his outpouring of gratitude to God. His thankfulness often carried him through the hardest of situations.

Thankfulness is a habit created through practice. I'm sure your mom had to remind you at times to say thank you after receiving a gift. Sometimes you need to be reminded to give thanks to God, especially during difficult days. In the midst of stress, disappointment, sadness, or great joy, the Lord deserves your praise and thanksgiving.

Part of God's plan and hope for your life is that you would choose to see the good and turn your complaints to praise. The more you think about God's goodness and practice giving thanks, the more it will naturally flow out of a genuine heart.

Think About It

What are things you can thank God for in your life?
What are some complaints you could turn into praise?

My Decrees

- I decree that I will cultivate a heart of thankfulness by giving Him thanks, no matter what is going on.

- I decree that I will praise Him because He is worthy.

- I declare that I will bless the Lord with a grateful heart.

- Thank You, Lord. I rejoice in who You are.

HUMILITY

"He guides the humble in what is right and teaches them his way."
(Psalm 25:9 NIV)

I t's natural to focus on yourself and things you want and need. It's easy to get wrapped up with problems you may face or things you don't like at the moment. When you become mostly focused on yourself, you can become self-absorbed. However, Jesus teaches a different way to live. He teaches us to be humble, which means focusing on others instead of solely on yourself.

Before coming to earth, Jesus lived in Heaven with His Father. He was, and is, King over the universe. He created the world. Yet when Jesus came to earth, He was born in a stable. He never became an earthly king. He was humble in every sense of the word. Jesus didn't come to earth to live like a king; He came to give His life for us. He knew that He was the King. He knew that He was and is our Lord, yet He came to serve. That is true humility. To be like Christ, you must do the same.

My Decrees

- I decree that I will not make everything about me!

- I decree that I will humble myself and serve others.

- I declare that I will keep His Word and His heart at the very center of my life.

- Thank You for being such a great example of humility.

20 READING THE BIBLE

"I have hidden your word in my heart,
that I might not sin against you."
(Psalm 119:11 NLT)

Reading the Bible is one of the most important things you can do. The Bible is God's Word, and all Scripture is "God-breathed." That means it is all from God and it's all useful and true.

You don't read the Bible just because you are a Christian and it's the right thing to do. You read it to know God more completely. It's a way to learn, love, trust, and be more like Him. God reveals Himself to you through His Word.

The Bible also gives you important instructions for how to live your life. When you read God's Word, it's important that you don't take things out of context or forget about the issues that you don't agree with. If the Bible says something that goes against what you believe, then you need to adjust your life to fit what Scripture says, not try to adjust what Scripture says to fit your life.

One of the best things you can do with Scripture is memorize it. When you hide God's Word in your heart, it will always be there for when you need it most. Pick up your Bible. Read it, learn it, and live it!

Think About It

**Why is it important to read your Bible?
What should you think if the Bible says
something you don't agree with?**

My Decrees

- I decree that I will make time every day to read and meditate on God's Word.

- I decree that no matter what I am going through, I will seek out the solution in the Bible.

- I decree that I will let my faith rise by speaking His Word into every situation.

- I declare that I will hide His Word in my heart.

- Thank You that Your Word never fails.

21 NOT TOO YOUNG

"'O Sovereign Lord,' I said, 'I can't speak for You! I'm too young!' The Lord replied, 'Don't say, "I'm too young," for you must go wherever I send you and say whatever I tell you.'"

(Jeremiah 1:6-7 NLT)

D o you ever wonder how you can be used for God right now or if there is something you could be doing that someone older and wiser couldn't? The truth is God not only can but also wants to use you. All He needs from you is a willing heart.

I recently was out for dinner and the waitress shared that she was feeling overwhelmed about some personal problems. I simply said, "I'll pray for you." She smiled and thanked me, and I noticed that her steps seemed lighter. I didn't make it weird; I didn't even pray with her in the restaurant. It seemed to be enough for her to know someone cared enough to pray.

Just as God used me, God wants to use you as well. There are many people around us that need us to step out and be God's hands and feet. Look for opportunities that He places in your life each day and see what God will do through you!

Think About It

Can you think of a time God prompted you to do something? In what ways could God use you right now?

My Decrees

- I decree that I will teach with my life and not allow anyone to put me down because of my youth.

- I decree that God wants to use me and will open doors so this can happen, even on a daily basis, in big ways and small ways.

- I decree that I will be an example because of the way I live my life by love, by faith, and by my character.

- I decree that I will cultivate these things and will not be distracted.

- I declare that I will be assisted by angels.

- Thank You, Lord, for working through me.

TRAINING YOUR THOUGHTS

"And now, dear brothers and sisters, one final thing. Fix your thoughts on what is true, and honorable, and right, and pure, and lovely, and admirable. Think about things that are excellent and worthy of praise."
(Philippians 4:8 NLT)

What if you kept a journal of the thoughts you had this past week? Would a pattern emerge? Did you have mostly good thoughts or did you record a lot of worries? God gave us the power to choose how our thoughts influence us.

What you think about, you become. If you are thinking about problems, then worry will fill your heart. If you are focused on sad stories and situations, you may feel depressed. The world is filled with things that try to have a place in your mind, such as cell phones, computers, streaming shows, or social media. Because of that, it is easy only to think on things the world tells you.

Thankfully, the Bible gives you the key against wrong thinking. It says to fix your thoughts on what is true, honorable, right, pure, lovely, and admirable. Be intentional and train your thoughts to think on the truths from God's word.

Think About It

What are some good things God wants you to think about? What can you do to train your thoughts?

My Decrees

- I decree that I will train myself to fill my mind and heart with good things, not things that can bring me down.

- I decree that I will search out God's Word if I am having wrong thoughts and ask Him to help me replace those thoughts with His.

- I decree that I will be careful what I allow to enter my soul and spirit, knowing it can affect me for good or for bad.

- I decree that I choose good.

- Thank You, Lord, for helping me to control my thoughts.

23
SPIRITUAL AUTHORITY

"I have given you authority to trample on snakes and scorpions and to overcome all the power of the enemy; nothing will harm you."
(Luke 10:19 NIV)

A s a child of God, you also have authority in Christ. It is your connection, relationship, and dependence on Jesus that give you this authority. This means you have the right to use the power of God's Name when you pray.

God's authority is given and available to you to confront every enemy that rises up against you. You can use your spiritual authority and claim victory over any situation. Anything that lines up with the Word of God can be declared over your life.

For example, Psalm 91 promises protection over you, so you use the authority you have in Jesus to declare protection over yourself. That same Psalm promises health; you have authority through Jesus over sickness and disease. As a child of God, you can command it to *go* in Jesus's Name.

The Name of Jesus is powerful because we are talking about the Person, Jesus Christ, His character, and the things He does. As believers, we know there is power in His Name because of who He is. Trust that as you pray in His Name, His power will be released in the situation.

Think About It

What are some things you can pray about in Jesus's Name? What do you have authority over because of Jesus?

My Decrees

- I decree that Jesus lives in me and by His Name and His power, I can exercise authority over any evil thing that tries to come against me.

- I declare His Word over every situation in my life and no weapon against me will prosper in the Name of Jesus.

- I decree that I will live and move and have my being in and through Him, and because of who He is I will see victory.

- Thank You for the power and authority I have in Your Name.

Dreaming Big

"God has given each of you a gift from his great variety of spiritual gifts. Use them well to serve one another."
(1 Peter 4:10 NLT)

God has given you gifts and abilities and He wants you to use them! Gifts and talents should be used to further the Kingdom of God, but often, we are too afraid to step out and use them.

Jesus told a parable about a master with three servants. To each of his servants, he gave a number of talents. Today, we use the word *talent* to mean something you are good at, but in Bible days *talent* meant a lot of money, like a big bag of gold. Two of the servants used their talents to make more money, but one of them buried his because he was afraid. When the master returned, he was very happy with the servants who had used what they were given, and very displeased with the servant who had hid his away.

Stepping out in faith and using the talents God has given you can be scary. Maybe you have a beautiful singing voice, but you're afraid of singing in front of people. Even if you fail the first time, you're not really failing because you have stepped out in faith. You are doing what God has called you to do, and He will bless your efforts. Dream big!

My Decrees

- I decree that I will not be limited in my dreams of how God can use me.

- I decree that I will seek Him to show me ways I can step out and serve others and trust Him to open the right doors at the right time.

- I decree that I will do everything I can to prepare myself to be used by Him by developing the gifts and strengths He has blessed me with.

- Thank You for the gifts and talents You have given me.

GUARDING YOUR HEART

"Guard your heart above all else, for it determines the course of your life."
(Proverbs 4:23 NLT)

You put a lot of effort into protecting your body. You wear a seatbelt in the car, a helmet when riding your bike, and shoes to protect your feet. Have you given much thought to protecting your heart? The above Bible verse says to *"guard your heart above all else."* That means it's even more important than guarding your body.

Two of the most important ways to protect your heart is by filtering what you watch and listen to. Our heart absorbs what is put into it and it needs to be filled with things that are good and pleasing to God. Knowing how to guard your heart is actually pretty simple, but it can be hard to do sometimes. Ask God for the strength and grace to protect your heart. Your heart guides your life and needs to be protected so you can fulfill the purpose and plans God has for you.

Think About It

Why is guarding your heart important?
What are ways you can protect your heart?

My Decrees

- I decree search my heart, examine it, and find anything hidden within me that is not of You.

- I declare that I will not be distracted from You. I will allow You to have Your way in me.

- I declare that You will protect my heart from evil and help me live a holy life.

- Thank You for giving me wisdom to guard my heart.

26 CALLING

"Lead a life worthy of your calling, for you have been called by God."
(Ephesians 4:1 NLT)

You have probably wondered at some point what your calling is, what you're supposed to do when you're older. You know God created you for a purpose and has great plans for you. He has also placed a calling on your life. A calling is a divine invitation to employment, to vocation.

It can seem overwhelming at times to think about your future because you don't want to get it wrong. It's important to know God may call you to do different things throughout your life. For example, I went to college to become a teacher and I did that for many years. Then I became a stay-at-home mom. Now, I am a worship leader, songwriter, and author. Did changing my career several times mean I wasn't following God's plans for my life? No!

God may call you to many different things throughout your life. As long as you are following Jesus, He will lead you into all He has planned for you.

Think About It

What are some things you enjoy doing?
Do you have some ideas of what
God is calling you to do?

My Decrees

- I decree that I will use the talents and gifts You have given me to fulfill my calling.

- I decree that I will seek You, pursue You, and listen for Your voice as You direct my path.

- I decree that I will watch for the open doors You put before me.

- I decree that I will do my part by praying and preparing to be ready for Your leading.

- Thank You for helping me grow into Your calling for my life.

27

ZEAL

"And you must love the Lord your God with all your heart, all your soul, and all your strength."
(Deuteronomy 6:5 NLT)

When you really care about something, it is said that you are *all in*. You are often committed, passionate, loyal, heartfelt, and on fire for what or who you believe in the most. The Bible calls this "zeal."

Zeal means having energy or enthusiasm about one's faith. That's the kind of life God calls all Christians to live. It means you are committed to God's way of doing things, not your own, and are eager to embrace all that God wants to do in your life, even if that means surrender or sacrifice. God isn't calling you only to serve him a little bit or love Him half-heartedly; He wants you to fully live for Him every day and in every way.

You should be passionate about serving the Lord and it should show in your words and actions. Be passionate about God's Word. Be hungry for His presence. Be bold in sharing your faith. Your zeal for God will help you fulfill your destiny. Love Him with all your heart, soul, mind, and strength!

My Decrees

- I decree that I will keep my zeal and passion stirred up for You.

- I decree that I will keep You as my number one priority.

- I decree that I will discipline myself to keep doing what I know to do by praying and reading Your Word.

- Thank You for giving me passion and zeal to live for You.

28 PEACEMAKERS

"Blessed are the peacemakers, for they will be called children of God."
(Matthew 5:9 NIV)

It takes courage to be a peacemaker. A peacemaker lives differently, by choosing love instead of choosing a side. A peacemaker seeks reconciliation rather than revenge.

There is a story in the Bible about a good Samaritan. A Jewish man was beaten up, robbed, and left to die on the side of the road. A priest and a Levite both walked by and did nothing to save the poor man. Then a Samaritan, who was the Jews' worst enemy, came upon the Jewish man and went out of his way to take care of the injured man. This is an example of peacemaking.

The Samaritan had mercy on the man who was considered his enemy. Those who make peace are called children of God. We make peace with others when we choose to be kind, pure hearted, and merciful, even when the world would say we shouldn't. Anyone can fight or be mean, but it takes true courage and strength to stay peaceful.

Think About It

What does it look like to be a peacemaker? Have you ever diffused a situation by bringing peace?

My Decrees

- I decree that I am a peacemaker!

- I decree that I choose daily to walk in love and compassion, and I will resist anger and conflict.

- I decree that I will watch my words and endeavor to use words of kindness to everyone I encounter.

- I decree that I will represent Jesus in all my relationships.

- Thank You for using me as one of Your peacemakers.

THE POWER
OF PRAYER

*"The earnest prayer of a righteous person has
great power and produces wonderful results."*
(James 5:16 NLT)

You may think prayer is boring, but it is one of the most powerful tools you have as a Christian. You don't need to pray in a formal way, using a bunch of thees and thous. Prayer is simply talking to God about your concerns, thoughts, and feelings. God absolutely hears you when you pray and He eagerly waits for you to come to Him in prayer. You are His child and He loves spending time with you!

Prayer helps you focus on God and learn more about Him. You become friends with Him and He loves you unconditionally. Prayer is an important weapon in making right choices.

You want to stop cheating? Pray. Do you need to be more loving to your sibling? Pray. Nothing is too big or too hard for God. Pray for yourself, your family, your friends, your school, and your nation. When you pray, God takes action!

My Decrees

- I decree that I will pray first!

- I decree that no matter what the situation, I will seek You and trust You for the answer as You are my Provider.

- I declare that everything I have need of is found in You.

- I declare that as I seek You first, You will do more than I can ask or think and Your timing is perfect.

- I decree Your Word over me to prosper and be in health and I trust You to make all things beautiful in Your time.

- Thank You that You hear me when I pray.

30
LIVING GOD'S WAY

"Stay on the path that the Lord your God has commanded you to follow. Then you will live long and prosperous lives in the land you are about to enter and occupy."
(**Deuteronomy 5:33 NLT**)

One amazing reason you can trust the Bible is the proof that it works! Countless people have lived God's way and have incredible testimonies because of it. If you live your life God's way, you will have a life He planned and created just for you. Remember how unique you are and the time God spent in designing your purpose and destiny. It doesn't mean that you won't have any pain or struggles, but it does mean that you will be equipped to handle anything that comes your way.

No other religion or worldview can promise and deliver the peace, love, joy, and fulfillment that comes from a life lived in obedience to Jesus Christ. A life without God is empty and full of needless problems and pain. If you learn what God says in the Bible and commit yourself to His way of doing things, you will not be disappointed. Remember, you are incredibly special to God and He loves you very much!

My Decrees

- I decree that I will live my life in such a way that all who are around me will have no doubt that I belong to Jesus and serve Him alone.

- I decree that I will live my life with purpose and I will make a difference in the lives of others.

- I declare that I have been set apart, created on purpose, and I choose to live and move and have my being in Him and for Him.

- Thank You for the peace, love, and joy that comes from living Your way.

RECEIVE PROMISES

(Ages 7th Grade–12th Grade)

1 God Never Lies

"God is not a man, so he does not lie. He is not human, so he does not change his mind. Has he ever spoken and failed to act? Has he ever promised and not carried it through?"
(**Numbers 23:19 NLT**)

God has promised many things to those who believe in Him. His promises are powerful and comforting, giving hope and encouragement to your life. All throughout the Bible, God made promises to His people and was faithful to keep them.

You may have experience with people breaking their promises to you or changing their mind about something. The verse above clearly states that God is not a man, so He doesn't lie or change His mind. He has *never* broken a promise!

Your part in believing the promises of God is to trust Him. Trusting God starts with believing who He says He is. He is good, powerful, faithful, loving, and kind. The consistency of God's character allows you to be confident in His promises. Even if you don't see the promises come exactly when you want, trust that God has the perfect timeline for you. Keep your hope and faith in Him. Believe God will be true to His Word. He will never fail you!

Think About It

Why can you trust in God's promises?
How can you trust His Word?

My Decrees

- I decree that I will stir up the promises of God over my life.

- I decree that I will walk in the truth of His Word in me.

- I decree that I will speak His promises and be strong in them because they are powerful and He is faithful to perform them.

- I decree that God never lies!

- Thank You, God, for keeping Your Word.

2 HOLY SPIRIT

"For all who are led by the Spirit of
God are children of God."
(Romans 8:14 NLT)

In the Bible you see three distinct persons: the Father, the Son, and the Holy Spirit. Holy Spirit comes to reside in your heart when you accept Jesus as your Savior. Holy Spirit was sent as a Helper to believers in the place of Jesus after He physically left the earth.

Holy Spirit is your Comforter and Nurturer. He fills you with life and empowers you to live supernaturally. When you need help, you can listen to what He is saying in your heart. He is the One who convicts you of sin and guards you from evil. Holy Spirit will bring Scriptures to your mind when you need them and give you the words to say when you're not sure what to pray. He is also the One who gives spiritual gifts to every believer.

The closer you get to God, the more you will experience Holy Spirit. You need Holy Spirit in your life!

Think About It
Who is Holy Spirit?
How does Holy Spirit help you?

My Decrees

- I decree that Holy Spirit is activated in my life and helps to lead and guide me into all truth.

- I decree that the anointing of Holy Spirit marks me and gives me power to live for You.

- I declare that I will listen for Holy Spirit direction, I will be comforted, and I will be empowered because Holy Spirit lives in me.

- Thank You for leading and guiding my life.

3 FRUIT OF THE SPIRIT

"But the Holy Spirit produces this kind of fruit in our lives: love, joy, peace, patience, kindness, goodness, faithfulness, gentleness, and self-control. There is no law against these things!" (Galatians 5:22-23 NLT)

The fruit of the Spirit is a gift from God to believers to help them live in ways that please Him and show His love to others. One role of Holy Spirit is guiding you to spiritual maturity. He helps transform your thoughts and actions to be more like Jesus. How do you know if you're growing and becoming more like Him?

The Bible says you can track your growth by the fruit of the Spirit. You can see Holy Spirit growing and changing you by the fruit you produce. You will produce certain words, thoughts, and actions. The fruit of the Spirit grows in you just as fruit grows on trees. When you put your faith in Jesus you are immediately forgiven of sin, but there is still a process of learning to be more like Christ. Holy Spirit helps us to make those changes. You will see the effect of those changes with the fruit you produce. Those who love Jesus will produce fruit that looks like Him.

Think About It

How do you get the fruit of the Spirit in your life? How do you grow spiritual fruit?

My Decrees

- I decree that I am growing in my walk with Jesus because Holy Spirit is producing fruit in my life.

- I declare that His love in me causes me to change for the better and this is my desire.

- I decree that my words and actions will be a reflection of Your fruit in my life and I will keep reaching for higher levels in You.

- Thank You for the fruit of the Spirit.

4 LOVE

"Love is patient and kind. Love is not jealous or boastful or proud or rude. It does not demand its own way. It is not irritable, and it keeps no record of being wronged. It does not rejoice about injustice but rejoices whenever the truth wins out. Love never gives up, never loses faith, is always hopeful, and endures through every circumstance."
(1 Corinthians 13:4-7 NLT)

L*ove* is a commonly used word. I love this song. I love pizza. I love this sports team. With how often the word is used, you may forget the power of it. Love is the first fruit listed in the fruit of the Spirit.

First Corinthians 13 is often referred to as "the love chapter" and gives some great insight into the love of God. God showed His great love for you by sending His son, Jesus, to die on the Cross for your sins. That is a powerful love. One of the most important characteristics of a Christian is to show God's love. In fact, it has been said that people will know you are a Christian by your love. It is a fruit, indicating the presence of the Holy Spirit.

There are many ways to show God's love to others such as being generous, kind, thoughtful, and encouraging. Try your best to show God's love in all you do!

Think About It

How can you show God's love to others? Why is love important?

My Decrees

- I decree that the overwhelming love of God operates in my life, filling me and changing me to be like Him.

- I declare that Your unfailing love transforms me and every day I become more like You in actions and words.

- I declare that I will show Your love to every person I encounter and in every situation I will seek love first.

- Thank You for Your love.

5 JOY

"Your statutes are my heritage forever;
they are the joy of my heart."
(Psalm 119:111 NIV)

Joy is another awesome fruit of the Spirit. Many confuse joy with happiness, but joy is much different. Happiness comes from what you are enjoying in the moment or if you've had a great day. It can shift with your mood and circumstances. Joy isn't dependent on your feelings or situation; it is grounded in God. So how do you find joy?

Joy is found in knowing Jesus. His joy is a gift you can choose to accept, no matter where you are in life. Psalm 16:11 mentions finding joy in God's presence. Jesus is your source of joy, so nothing can take that away. You can even have joy in times of sadness or confusion. You cannot be happy in times of sadness, but you can have joy.

Grow yourself in God through reading His Word and spending time with Him and your fruit of joy will also grow. Joy comes from knowing, believing, and trusting in God. When your joy comes from God, nothing can stop it!

Think About It

How is joy different from happiness?
Why can you have joy in any situation?

My Decrees

- I decree that I have Your joy living in me!

- I decree that I will face every situation from a place of joy and peace because that is where my strength comes from.

- I declare that You are all I need and I will press more and more into You where joy is made complete, which enables me to face every situation.

- Thank You for Your joy.

6 PEACE

"And let the peace that comes from Christ rule in your hearts. For as members of one body you are called to live in peace. And always be thankful."
(Colossians 3:15 NLT)

Peace is a wonderful gift as a result of the Holy Spirit being in your life. It is easy to fill your days with anxious thoughts, stress, and fear. Biblical peace is completely opposite of all these feelings! It is the absence of stress, worry, fear, and chaos.

Peace in God means you can rest in His presence as you remember who He is and trust in Him completely. There may be things you enjoy that bring you peace such as listening to music, reading a book, or going for a walk, but those peaceful times end. The peace of God never ends and is always available to you.

You will experience the peace of God as you remember He keeps His promises and He is in control of every part of your life. His Spirit is in you, producing the fruit of peace. Rest in Him. There is nothing in the world that could ever compare to the biblical peace of God!

Think About It

What is God's peace? How is God's peace different from the world's view?

My Decrees

- I decree that peace comes even when I don't understand everything going on around me.

- I decree that my heart is fixed on You and I will not worry or be anxious or try to figure things out on my own, but I will rest in You and let peace take control.

- I declare that I will have peace in Your presence.

- Thank You for Your peace.

7 PATIENCE

"Wait patiently for the Lord. Be brave and courageous. Yes, wait patiently for the Lord."
(Psalm 27:14 NLT)

Being patient is hard. It would be surprising to hear someone say he enjoys waiting. Most things in life are available quickly: fast food, online orders delivered in a day, instant test results, and even access to shows to watch whenever you want. However, not everything in life is fast. Have you ever prayed and asked God for something and then waited and waited, wondering if you would ever get the answer or results?

Being patient is tough and it requires great trust in God. But since patience is a fruit of the Spirit, you know God wants you to have it. He will help you develop patience in your life.

Don't be discouraged if you are still waiting on an answer to a prayer. Take the opportunity to ask God to help you with patience. Remember, God will not let you down; it just may take time. Patiently trust God. He will come through for you!

Think About It

Is there anything you are waiting on from God?
How can you develop patience in your life?

My Decrees

- I decree that I will let patience work in me, I will be brave, and I will trust in the perfect timing of the Lord.

- I declare that You are faithful to keep every promise and my part is to be patient in the waiting.

- I declare that I will allow patience to grow in me, knowing You are the Author and the Finisher of my faith.

- I declare that I will be patient!

- Thank You for Your patience.

8 KINDNESS

"Be kind to one another, tenderhearted, forgiving one another, as God in Christ forgave you."
(Ephesians 4:32 ESV)

Kindness is a characteristic that God wants you to have. It is defined as being friendly, generous, and considerate. If you are living according to God's Word, then kindness will be a fruit that grows out of your life. No one is kind all the time but the more you know God the more you become like Him. God will give you the power to be kind and kindness will become part of your character.

One of the ways you can show kindness is through your words. Simply ask yourself if what you are about to say is kind. If it is, say it! If it's not, change it! Actions are another way you can show kindness. Take time to purposefully make sure your actions are kind. You can also show kindness with your attitude. When a situation happens that makes you feel irritated or angry, choose to react with kindness.

Kindness is important to God. If you are struggling, ask Him to help you. Remember, it never hurts to be kind!

Think About It

**Do you think others would describe
you as kind? Why or why not?
How can you show kindness to others?**

My Decrees

- I decree that kindness is a fruit of the Spirit that operates in me and through me.

- I declare Your grace over me to help me be tender and loving, walking in forgiveness, just like I would like to be treated.

- I declare that I will use my actions to display Your lovingkindness to all I encounter and I will watch my words and attitude to be sure they line up with who You are.

- Thank You for Your kindness.

9 GOODNESS

"So let's not get tired of doing what is good. At just the right time we will reap a harvest of blessing if we don't give up."
(Galatians 6:9 NLT)

As a Christian, you have been called to a life of goodness. Goodness refers to your morals and values, who you are. When you are filled with the Spirit, this fruit begins growing in your life and becomes part of your nature. You want to be good because that is what God is.

One of the most important beliefs of a Christian is that God is always good. God has promised His goodness to you. This means anything that happens in your life, good or bad, God will work it for good. This is such an important truth for you to know.

If you are going through a tough time, remember the goodness of God. You are also called to *do* good. Show compassion and forgiveness to others. When you draw closer to Jesus and get to know Him more and more, the fruit of the Spirit becomes part of who you are, and goodness will flow out of you.

My Decrees

- I decree that goodness follows after me and operates within me.

- I take authority over any weariness that would try to keep me from doing what is good and I will not give up!

- I declare that God is good and I will live by His morals and values.

- I declare that goodness flows through me to others and as I grow in You, goodness abounds more and more.

- Thank You for Your goodness.

10 FAITHFULNESS

"But be sure to fear the Lord and faithfully serve him. Think of all the wonderful things he has done for you."
(1 Samuel 12:24 NLT)

Faithfulness is a fruit of the Spirit and is a result of the Spirit working in your life. Faithfulness is loyalty to a God who has never let you down. He has proven Himself trustworthy time and time again. Believing that God is who He says He is and He keeps His promises produces faithfulness.

Throughout the Bible there are many stories of individuals who were faithful to God. Noah built an ark for rain that no one believed would come, but he had faith because God said it. Abraham and Sarah believed God would give them a child, even though they were very old. They trusted God because they knew God to be faithful.

God has never *not* been faithful, so you can trust Him with your life and be faithful to Him and His Word. As you live your life according to His ways, the fruit of the Spirit will grow in you. He's worthy and deserving of your faithfulness!

Think About It

How can God's faithfulness be seen in your life?
How can you show your faithfulness to God?

My Decrees

- I decree that I am growing in faithfulness, true to my Father who never lets me down and keeps every promise.

- I decree that I pledge my allegiance to You and proclaim You are greater than any problem or distraction.

- I decree that because of Your faithfulness, I will be loyal, devoted, trustworthy, steadfast, and true.

- Thank You for Your faithfulness.

11

GENTLENESS

"Let your gentleness be evident
to all. The Lord is near."
(Philippians 4:5 NIV)

Gentleness is a fruit of the Spirit that causes you to be kind and compassionate to others. Gentleness is not to be confused with weakness. It is a strong hand with a soft touch. Gentleness is similar to kindness, but it involves having a softness of heart toward other people.

Jesus wants you to be gentle with your words, actions, and attitudes. He models gentleness throughout the Bible. He consistently shows kindness and mercy to others, showing how He desires you to live. Describing God as gentle does not mean He is not powerful. God is always there for you, caring, protecting, and guiding you.

Gentleness requires humility, sacrifice, patience, and compassion. Serve Jesus with intention, opening yourself up to the Spirit and all the gifts. He knows that the greatest and most important plans can come to fruition when they are carried out with gentleness.

Think About It

Is gentleness a part of who you are right now?
How can you show gentleness to others?

My Decrees

- I decree that I will submit my heart to You every day and allow You to keep it clean so that I will be gentle and kind to others.

- I declare that I will show Your mercy and kindness and display Your love and power to others so they are drawn by Your Spirit to know You.

- I declare that Your gentleness lives in me and through me.

- Thank You for Your gentleness.

12

SELF-CONTROL

"A person without self-control is like
a city with broken-down walls."
(Proverbs 25:28 NLT)

Many things in life require self-control. Self-control is essentially being in charge of your words, thoughts, feelings, and actions. It is being able to respond to things rather than react to them.

God doesn't want you to live angry, upset, and stressed out; He wants you full of self-control. Proverbs 25:28 says if you don't have self-control, you are *"like a city with broken-down walls."* A city surrounded with walls is protected from an enemy's attack. If an enemy was able to knock the walls down, the city would be left unprotected. If the city's walls were never rebuilt, the enemy could always get in. So, if you don't have self-control, this means you don't have any protection against the temptation to sin. Self-control helps you resist temptation by knowing and doing what is right.

As a child of God, you've got Holy Spirit living inside you. He's there to help you and lead you into making good decisions.

Think About It

How can you practice self-control in your life?
How does having self-control help you?

My Decrees

- I decree that I will take responsibility for exercising self-control in and through my life, developing it more and more in order to grow up in You.

- I declare that I will read Your Word, pray in the Spirit, and build a wall of protection against temptation to sin.

- I declare that I will trust You to help me with this as I submit myself to You.

- Thank You for helping me develop self-control.

13 PROTECTION

"This I declare that about the Lord: He alone is my refuge, my place of safety; he is my God, and I trust him."
(Psalm 91:2 NLT)

God protects those who love Him and follow His ways. Psalm 91 says He is your refuge. That means He is your place of safety. He's the One you cry out and talk to when you are feeling scared or fearful.

Have you ever been inside, enjoying safety and protection while a storm raged outside? You probably felt good knowing you were protected. That is what Psalm 91 says about God. He is your shelter and protection in life's storms. He also says His angels will help guard you. What a promise!

As you grow your relationship with God through reading your Bible, praying, and worshipping Him, He will wrap His arms around you, keeping you safe and secure. The shelter of God is always stable and unshakeable. When He covers you with protection, no harm can get through to you. Though you're not promised a life without struggles or challenges, you are promised God will be there to protect and guard you. Trust and believe the promises of His protection!

Think About It
How does God protect you?
What does the Bible say about God's protection?

My Decrees

- I decree that You are my shield, my strong tower, and I am safe in the shelter of Your arms.

- I declare that angels are all around me and assisting in my protection and the enemy is defeated.

- I decree that I have Your strength to face any situation and You are the Rock on which I stand.

- Thank You for the promise of Your protection.

14 HEALING

"For I am the Lord who heals you."
(Exodus 15:26 NLT)

Go od is known by many names in the Bible and one of those is "Jehovah Rapha, the God who heals." It is important to believe and trust that God is your Healer. He not only heals physical needs but also spiritual, emotional, and mental needs.

In Bible times and today, some people are healed instantly and some are healed over time. When someone is made well instantly, that is referred to as a miracle. For example, if a person has been bound to a wheelchair for years and suddenly gets up and runs, that's a miracle! Other people may slowly get better over time. Both of these are awesome ways that Jesus heals.

If you have asked for healing in the past and haven't received it yet, ask again! The Bible says to ask and *"keep on asking"* (Matthew 7:7 NLT). Stir your faith up with the promises of God by praying and decreeing. Trust and believe in the God who heals!

Think About It

**How can you believe God for healing?
What if you have prayed for healing
and it hasn't happened yet?**

My Decrees

- I decree that You are my Healer.

- I decree that You are the God of miracles.

- I declare that You meet every need I could possibly have—spirit, soul, and body.

- I believe You died for my salvation and my healing. You are more than enough!

- Thank You for being Jehovah Rapha, the God who heals.

HOPE

"May the God of hope fill you with all joy and peace in believing, so that by the power of the Holy Spirit you may abound in hope."
(Romans 15:13 ESV)

Scripture consistently says your hope is in Jesus. Romans 5:5 (ICB) says, *"This hope will never disappoint us."*

In a passage about the confidence you can have in God's promises, Hebrews 6:18-19 mentions taking refuge by seizing the sure anchor of hope that is set before us. The hope you have in Jesus is an anchor to your soul. That means hope doesn't float on the surface of your situation but it gets down to the bottom and holds on tight.

Biblical hope is confident expectancy. The world defines hope as wishing something would happen. The world's definition says, "I hope this will happen, but I don't really know if it will." Biblical hope is much different. It is looking forward to something with absolute confidence, expecting fulfillment.

When you're tempted to be downcast by your circumstances, you can gain Heaven's perspective by looking up to God and being filled with the kind of hope that can only come from Him. Believe He has good things for you and place your hope in Him!

Think About It
Why can you place your hope in God?
How is hope an anchor to your soul?

My Decrees

- I decree that hope abounds in me and my heart overflows with great expectancy.

- I declare that Holy Spirit gives me the ability to walk in peace and joy in the waiting period.

- I decree that hope never disappoints.

- Thank You for filling me with hope.

16
GOD WORKS ALL FOR YOUR GOOD

"And we know that all things work together for good to them that love God, to them who are the called according to his purpose."
(Romans 8:28 KJV)

This verse is an amazing promise from God. You can be confident and strong in knowing and standing upon this truth. This verse says *"all things work together for good."* All means all!

However, that doesn't mean that everything in your life will be good. You will go through difficult times and you may experience sickness or loss. But this verse is a powerful promise that God will take those things and ultimately bring good out of them.

Think of Joseph in the Bible. His brothers were so jealous of him they threw him in a pit and then sold him as a slave. He was lied about and thrown in prison. But Joseph still became a ruler of the land, second only to Pharaoh. Joseph then made a powerful statement: *"You intended to harm me, but God intended it all for good"* (Exodus 50:20 NLT). Because Joseph loved and trusted God during his difficult times, God was able to turn his situation for good. If you love and trust God, He will do the same for you!

Think About It
**Have you ever gone through
a hard time that ultimately became good?
Why does God work things for your good?**

My Decrees

- I decree that I love You and I trust You to turn all things in my life for good. This is Your promise.

- I loose angels to assist however needed to bring this to pass.

- I declare that Your goodness is running after me and never gives up on me.

- I decree that the enemy is defeated and I declare that God of the turnaround operates in my life.

- Thank You for taking what was meant to harm me and turning it for good.

17
GOD WILL NEVER LEAVE YOU

"Be strong and brave. Don't be afraid of them. Don't be frightened. The Lord your God will go with you. He will not leave you or forget you."
(Deuteronomy 31:6 ICB)

God will never leave or forget you. This promise will help you face any fear or challenge in life. You can be confident knowing that God is always with you.

God first made this promise to the Israelites after He delivered them from Pharaoh's rule in Egypt. As they faced enemies that stood between them and the land promised to them by God, He made this vow to them. When Joshua took over leading the Israelites, God made this same promise to him. Over and over again, God repeated this promise. He wanted the children of Israel to trust that He would always be with them, no matter what. We see in His Word that He kept His promise. He was faithful to be there for the Israelites every step of the way.

This same promise has been made to you. Be strong and brave, trusting that God is always there for you. He will never leave or forget you.

Think About It

**What does this promise mean to you?
How can this promise help you be
brave and strong in a situation?**

My Decrees

- I decree that no matter what I see or feel, You are with me, a Friend that sticks closer than a brother.

- I decree that You never leave or forsake me.

- I declare that I have no fear because I am strong and brave because You keep Your Word and are with me every step I take.

- Thank You for always being there.

18
SPIRITUAL ARMOR

"Put on all of God's armor so that you will be able to stand firm against all strategies of the devil."
(Ephesians 6:11 NLT)

This verse says you must be prepared to fight in spiritual battles. God will help you stand against evil and He will defeat the powers of darkness. He gives you weapons to help you stand strong. You can see the weapons He provides in Ephesians 6.

The *"belt of truth"* helps you to be firmly grounded in the truth of Jesus and His Word. The *"breastplate of righteousness"* is doing what is right. Your *"feet shod with the gospel of peace"* means being ready to share the good news of Jesus with others. With the *"shield of faith"* you can go forth boldly. The *"helmet of salvation"* means Jesus has saved you from your sins. *"The sword of the Spirit"* represents the Word of God. The Word of God is a powerful weapon, especially when used under the power and guidance of Holy Spirit. With the full armor of God on, you will be able to stand and fight confidently in spiritual battles.

My Decrees

- I decree that I am equipped with the spiritual armor. You provide truth, doing what is right, sharing the gospel, faith, salvation, and Your Word.

- I decree that I will not fight as the world fights. I arm myself with spiritual weapons and I am armed and battle ready!

- I decree that I am more than a conqueror!

- Thank You for providing all I need to stand against the enemy.

ANGELS

"Beware that you don't look down on any of these little ones. For I tell you that in heaven their angels are always in the presence of my heavenly Father."
(Matthew 18:10 NLT)

ngels are one of the greatest benefits God has given you. Did you realize guardian angels are actually real? Angels are plural in the above verse, meaning you have at least two guardian angels assigned to your life. There is no Scripture in the entire Bible that indicates you ever lose these angels.

Before there was ever one day to your life, God wrote down plans and the destiny He had in mind for you. God has great plans for you. Your future is bright, and your destiny is good. There are no disasters planned by God for your life. The enemy may have some planned, but God does not. His plans are only good and filled with hope.

The angels assigned to your life most certainly know about your destiny. The angels who are in Heaven in the presence of Jesus are also taught by Him concerning your purpose. You have an amazing destiny written by God Himself, and angels are assigned to help you fulfill it!

My Decrees

- I decree that the angels assigned to my life are assisting me to walk out the plan and purpose for my life.

- I declare that I will accomplish my destiny as angels accompany me and help me.

- I declare that angels keep me from falling into traps, keep me from stumbling, and keep the enemy under my feet!

- Thank You, God, for helping me complete my destiny.

GRACE

"God saved you by his grace when you believed. And you can't take credit for this; it is a gift from God."
(Ephesians 2:8 NLT)

Grace is God's unmerited favor to believers. It is an incredible gift and promise of God. Everyone has sinned and falls short of the standards of God. The cost of God's grace was the life of His Son, Jesus, on the Cross.

Jesus came to the earth to remove your sins and to make you right with God. If your sins could be removed by doing good works, then there would be no need for Jesus to come. What Jesus did was given to you freely. You didn't have to earn it; you simply have to believe in Jesus. The grace of God isn't based on what you can do, but rather in what Jesus has already done.

God's grace is strong enough to help you with any struggle you may face. God also wants you to extend grace by forgiving others. Grace is amazing. All throughout the Bible, it shows you a God who pursues and loves you. Thank God for His grace!

Think About It
What does the gift of grace mean?
How can you show grace to others?

My Decrees

- I decree that even when I don't deserve it, You still pour out Your grace over me and give me mercy, new every morning.

- I declare that Your grace is greater than anything I've ever done and I will do my best to extend it to others.

- I decree that the gift of grace is strong in me and helps me with any struggles I have.

- Thank You for Your amazing grace.

HEARING GOD'S VOICE

"My sheep listen to my voice; I know them, and they follow me."
(John 10:27 NLT)

There are many voices you can choose to listen to through the news, social media, friends, and others. The most important voice to listen and follow is God's.

How do you know the voice of your best friend so well? Because you spend so much time together. You can have the same experience and relationship with God. The more you spend time with Him, the more you will recognize and know His voice. One of the best ways to hear God is from reading the Bible. The Bible is God's Word and He speaks to you through it.

Another way God speaks to you is through thoughts and ideas He puts in your head. For example, if someone's name comes into your mind, it might be God's way of telling you to pray for that person. If a Bible verse comes to your mind, God may be encouraging you with it or telling you do what the verse says.

It is important to know the voice of God you're trying to hear will never go against what the Bible says. If you have a thought in your head that goes against the Bible, then that's not God. Take time to listen for God's voice; He promises you will hear from Him.

My Decrees

- I decree that I will press in to know You more and hear Your voice more clearly than I ever have before.

- I declare that I will only follow Your voice and not the voice of a stranger.

- I decree that Your voice will speak to me through Your Word and in prayer.

- Thank You for helping me recognize Your voice.

22 RAINBOW PROMISE

"I have placed my rainbow in the clouds. It is the sign
of my covenant with you and with all the earth."
(Genesis 9:13 NLT)

The brightest rainbows appear after the darkest storms. When facing a challenge, remember the promise of the rainbow through the Bible story of Noah. The entire population of the world had become so evil and wicked that God decided to bring a flood to the earth to destroy everyone except Noah and his family. God instructed Noah to build an ark that was big enough to hold one male and one female from every kind of animal and creature. It rained for 40 days and nights and water flooded the earth. When the rain finally stopped and the land was dry enough, Noah and his family left the ark and let all the animals out to find a new home. Noah built an altar and thanked God for taking care of them. God made Noah a promise He would never flood the earth again and put a bright rainbow in the sky as a reminder of His promise.

Just as God guided Noah and kept him safe, He will guide you through life's uncertainties. When you see a rainbow, you can be reminded that God is faithful to His Word.

Think About It
What is God's rainbow promise?
How can you trust God through life's storms?

My Decrees

- I decree that You are my ark of safety in times of uncertainty.

- I declare that when doubt tries to flood my mind, I will be reminded instead of the power and promise of God to lead me through to great victory.

- I decree that Your rainbow is a sign of Your faithfulness that bad times will end.

- Thank You for the reminder of Your promise.

23 STRENGTH

"Each time he said, 'My grace is all you need. My power works best in weakness.' So now I am glad to boast about my weaknesses, so that the power of Christ can work through me. That's why I take pleasure in my weaknesses, and in the insults, hardships, persecutions, and troubles that I suffer for Christ. For when I am weak, then I am strong."
(2 Corinthians 12:9-10 NLT)

In these verses Paul is not boasting about his greatness; he is boasting about his weaknesses! That's the opposite of what most people do. The Bible doesn't say what Paul's problems were, but it does say he asked God many times to take them away. However, instead of removing the problems, God said His grace would be all Paul needed. That caused Paul to respond by calling his problems a good thing.

Do you think your struggles can sometimes be a good thing? Paul wasn't the only one in the Bible who faced difficulties. When God called Moses to lead the Israelites, Moses said he wasn't a good speaker and couldn't do it. God reminded Moses He would provide Moses with all he needed. Where Moses was weak, God was stronger. God didn't remove the problems for Paul and Moses, but their attitudes changed.

God can, and will, sometimes remove your problems when you pray, but other times He promises His grace will help you go through them. God's promise to Paul and Moses is also a promise for you. When you are weak, He is strong. Find your strength in Him!

Think About It

**How can God make you strong
when you're feeling weak? Why doesn't
God always take away your problems?**

My Decrees

- I decree that I can do all things through Christ who strengthens me.

- I decree that it is Your power who works in me to help me when I feel weak.

- I declare that Your grace is greater than any of my problems and I will keep my attitude straight.

- Thank You that when I am weak, You are strong.

OVERCOMER

"I have told you all this so that you may have peace in me. Here on earth you will have many trials and sorrows. But take heart, because I have overcome the world."
(John 16:33 NLT)

Some of the last words Jesus spoke on the earth are found in John 16. Jesus was speaking to His disciples and reassuring them of what would be taking place with His death and resurrection. He then told them, *"Take heart, because I have overcome the world."*

There is no doubt there are many troubles in the world today. You may also be facing personal struggles. Jesus wants you to have peace amid any difficulties. This verse doesn't say you won't have trouble but it does promise He will be there for you. You don't have to face anything alone.

Take heart means to be confident in a hard situation. You can be courageous because Jesus showed you how to be. He died on the Cross and rose again three days later, proving that He can overcome anything! *Overcome* means to win over something. You can overcome situations by placing your faith in Jesus, knowing that your victory is in Him.

Think About It

**How does God help you overcome troubles?
How can you have peace amid struggles?**

My Decrees

- I decree that I overcome through the blood of Jesus and through my testimony of what You have done for me.

- I decree that nothing can overtake me. You give Your angels charge over me.

- I declare that Your Word says I am strong and in You I have the victory.

- I decree that I am coming over!

- Thank You for making me an overcomer.

ABUNDANT LIFE

"The thief comes only to steal and kill and destroy. I came that they may have life and have it abundantly."
(John 10:10 ESV)

Jesus promises you an abundant life. *Abundant* is the Greek word *perisson*, which means something that is "exceedingly, very highly, beyond measure, more, a quantity including so much more than what we could ever expect or anticipate."[1] This means Jesus gives you more than you can ever imagine. He has a wonderful hope and future in place for you.

This verse also says that trouble doesn't come from God. Things that steal and destroy are from the devil. Jesus doesn't want to harm you. If you're in the middle of a hard situation, be encouraged that God will be close to you. He wants you to be filled with His peace and presence.

There is a big difference between worldly abundance and spiritual abundance. Worldly abundance includes many material items. The abundant life given to you by God comes when you accept Jesus as your Savior. It has to do with the love, joy, and peace you find in your heart and life as you begin to follow and grow in the Lord. Live abundantly in Him!

My Decrees

- I decree that abundance is overflowing and overtaking me. My cup runs over because of Your lovingkindness.

- I decree that I walk in peace and joy because of Your blessings and benefits.

- I declare that the enemy cannot steal any of God's promises from me and I will walk in the fullness of Your Word.

- I declare life and life abundantly!

- Thank You for an abundant life.

26 REDEMPTION

"In him we have redemption through his blood, the forgiveness of sins, in accordance with the riches of God's grace."
(Ephesians 1:7 NIV)

Redemption is a powerful promise of God to deliver you from the power of sin. Redemption is when God takes something bad and turns it into something good. God loves to redeem painful, sad, broken times and make them better. Redemption can also be thought of as an exchange or paying a price for something.

Jesus paid the price for your sin and punishment through his death and resurrection. The Bible is very clear that redemption from sins is only available through the blood of Jesus. When you invite Jesus into your life, He takes away your sins, redeeming your heart into a pure one. God also redeems the bad in your life. You can be held captive to things such as fear, hurt, regret, or emotional scars. God wants you free from such things, so He will redeem them and make them good. He can turn fear to bravery, hurt to deliverance and hopelessness to hope. Jesus is your Redeemer!

My Decrees

- I decree that sin has no hold on me, my Redeemer is alive and well, and He makes all things new.

- I declare that because He died for me, He has forgiven me and cleansed me.

- I decree that He has set me free and given me a new heart.

- I declare that He no longer sees the "old" me. He sees Jesus in me!

- Thank You for redeeming me through Your blood.

27 FORGIVENESS

"But if we confess our sins to him, he is faithful and just to forgive us our sins and to cleanse us from all wickedness."

(1 John 1:9 NLT)

Have you ever done something wrong and needed to ask for forgiveness? It is such a big relief when someone offers you forgiveness. God promises forgiveness to you. Forgiveness of sin is only possible through the blood of Jesus.

Some sins may feel too great. You may be tempted to try to hide them from God. God knows everything, so it's best to just be honest. There is no sin outside of God's ability to forgive. He will forgive you completely and He will also forgive you repeatedly.

As God has forgiven you, He wants you to forgive others. He wants you to release any feelings of hurt and blame. He desires for you to be forgiving, merciful, and kind to people. It may be hard for you to forgive and forget, but Jesus says in Psalm 103 that He does just that. Once He's forgiven you, He chooses not to remember your sin! God's forgiveness is a powerful promise. He loves you and is waiting for you with open arms.

Think About It
Why should you ask God for forgiveness?
Why should you forgive others?

My Decrees

- I decree that I walk in the promise of God. If I sin and I repent and turn to Him, He forgives and restores me.

- I declare that He loves and forgives me and sets me on a solid path.

- I decree that I can choose to forgive others because of His forgiveness extended toward me.

- Thank You for being faithful and just to forgive me of my sins.

SALVATION

"For God so loved the world that He gave His only begotten Son, that whoever believes in Him should not perish but have everlasting life."

(John 3:16 NKJV)

The promise of salvation is a beautiful gift from God. God's heart is that everyone would accept Jesus as their Lord. He loves you so much that He gave His Son for you. Because Jesus took your place, you now have a way to have a relationship with God and a way to Heaven.

God not only wants you to get saved, He desires that you know Him. The way of salvation is only through Jesus and it is actually very simple to do! The first step in salvation is to admit you are a sinner. Jesus said, *"Repent, for the kingdom of heaven is at hand,"* in Matthew 4:17 (NKJV). *Repent* means to turn and go the other way. Turn from your sin, and begin doing what is right in the eyes of God. Ask Him for forgiveness. Believe in your heart that Jesus died for your sins and confess that He is Lord.

Living a life for God is key to unlocking your full potential and destiny.

Think About It

What does salvation mean?
How can you be saved?

My Decrees

- I decree that I am a child of God, my sins are forgiven, my heart is clean, and I am washed in the blood of the Lamb!

- I decree that I am no longer bound by chains to sin but I am free because You have saved me.

- I declare that I will walk in Your ways, on a firm foundation, and I will keep my eyes on You!

- Thank You for saving me.

SPIRITUAL
INHERITANCE

*"Now you are no longer a slave but
God's own child. And since you are his
child, God has made you his heir."*
(Galatians 4:7 NLT)

When you accept Jesus through the gift of salvation, you're adopted into God's family. You become a son or a daughter and are considered an heir. An heir is someone who has the right to receive another person's property after the person's death. As a believer you have the right to everything that God has. You have an incredible spiritual and eternal inheritance. What an amazing promise!

Every blessing, benefit, and promise in the Bible belongs to you. This includes peace, love, grace, wisdom, joy, victory, strength, guidance, mercy, forgiveness, righteousness, discernment, and every other spiritual benefit. You can talk and relate to God as a loving Father. Part of being a son or daughter of God is to share His love and goodness with others. It also includes being bold in your faith and defending God's Kingdom. After all, it's your Kingdom too, as you have an inheritance in it!

Remember, you are God's child and your value is priceless.

Think About It
What does being a child of God mean?
What is a spiritual inheritance?

My Decrees

- I decree that I belong to God's family and I am a rightful heir to all His promises.

- I claim my inheritance from Him and I walk in every benefit He has provided.

- I declare His fullness over my life and I pledge to share with others how incredible it is to belong to Him!

- Thank You that I am an heir of God and a joint heir with Christ.

30 HEAVEN

"There is more than enough room in my Father's home. If this were not so, would I have told you that I am going to prepare a place for you?"
(John 14:2 NLT)

If you believe in Jesus, then Heaven is an incredible promise of God. The Bible gives some awesome descriptions of it. Heaven is a physical place with gardens, cities, kingdoms, and rivers. The most beautiful place on earth is just a glimpse of what Heaven will be like.

Jesus said He was going to prepare a room for you in His Father's house, which is Heaven. In Heaven you will still have your identity, memories, gifts, and passions that will be used for God's glory. God's glory is so bright that it stays light all the time. There will not be any pain, hurt, or tears in Heaven. Most importantly, Heaven is the dwelling place of God. He will be there and all your family and friends who believe in Jesus will be there too.

The book of Revelation describes Heaven as a place where the streets are paved with gold, the gates are made of pearl, and the walls made of precious jewels. As wonderful as you can imagine Heaven being, it will be far greater! Continue to trust, believe, and live for God, knowing that the promise of Heaven is yours.

Think About It
What do you think Heaven will be like?
What questions do you have about Heaven?

My Decrees

- I decree that Heaven is my eternal home and my destiny continues there.

- I declare that I will live for You, serve You, and rest in knowing You have already prepared a place for me.

- I decree that the best is yet to come!

- Thank You for the promise of Heaven!

31 DECREES FOR AMERICA

*"First, I tell you to pray for all people. Ask God
for the things people need, and be thankful
to him. You should pray for kings and for all
who have authority. Pray for the leaders so
that we can have quiet and peaceful lives—
lives full of worship and respect for God."*
(1 Timothy 2:1-2 ICB)

It is important to pray for your nation's leaders because they must make decisions every day. Their decisions should reflect God's morals and values. As a follower of Jesus, your prayer is powerful and effective. You can pray these decrees over America with the authority you have in Jesus. (If you live in another country, say the name of your country in place of *America*.)

My Decrees

- I decree that America is God's nation!

- I decree that we have no king but Jesus!

- I decree that America will reconnect to covenants between God and our founding fathers. Deep state corruption will be exposed!

- I decree that God will promote leaders who have His heart and remove those who do not!

- I decree that the church of King Jesus is rising in America to promote a righteous standard in all 50 states!

- I decree that the promotion of antichrist laws will be defeated. Laws based on God's principles will be promoted!

- I decree that the greatest revival in America's history will soon begin. Millions will come to Jesus!

- I declare that a cleansing of polluted values will come, and a moral compass will be restored!

- I declare that liberty and freedom provided by our Creator will not be taken from us!

- I declare that America shall be saved!

NOTES

1. G5249 – *perisson* (KJV). James Strong, *The New Strong's Exhaustive Concordance of the Bible* (Nashville, TN: Thomas Nelson Publishers, 1990).

ABOUT
DR. TIM SHEETS

Tim Sheets is an apostle, pastor of Oasis Church, founder of Awakening Now Prayer Network, and author. He travels extensively throughout the nations, carrying His heart and vision for awakening and reformation, the coming generation, and releasing an anointing for signs, wonders, and miracles. He and his wife, Carol, reside in Lebanon, Ohio.

ABOUT
RACHEL SHAFER

Rachel Shafer is an author, worship leader, songwriter, and speaker. Her book, *Expect God*, answers the question of what to do when your problem is hiding your promise. Her message is one of hope and expectation in life's unexpected moments. Rachel has released many recording projects with Oasis Worship with the most recent release including "I'll Be The One," "God of Breakthrough," and "War Cry." She also released "America's Anthem," a song filled with prayers and decrees over our nation. Rachel resides in Ohio with her husband and four children.

CONTACT INFORMATION FOR TIM SHEETS

Tim Sheets Ministries

www.timsheets.org

6927 Lefferson Road
Middletown, Ohio 45044

carol@timsheets.org

513.424.7150

 Facebook.com/ApostleTimSheets

 @TimDSheets

Contact Information for Rachel Shafer

Rachel Shafer Ministries

www.rachelshafer.com

6927 Lefferson Road
Middletown, Ohio 45044

rshafer4@gmail.com

513.424.7150

 Facebook.com/RachelNShafer

 @RShafer4

YOUR
Prophetic
C O M M U N I T Y

Are you passionate about hearing God's voice, walking with Jesus, and experiencing the power of the Holy Spirit?

Destiny Image is a community of believers with a passion for equipping and encouraging you to live the prophetic, supernatural life you were created for!

We offer a fresh helping of practical articles, dynamic podcasts, and powerful videos from respected, Spirit-empowered, Christian leaders to fuel the holy fire within you.

Sign up now to get awesome content delivered to your inbox
destinyimage.com/sign-up

 Destiny Image